The Custody Minefield

Parental Separation
Your Rights and the Law

Michael Robinson

ORANA
PUBLISHING

First published in Great Britain in 2006 by Orana Publishing Limited
www.oranapublishing.com

A CIP catalogue record for this book is available from the British Library.

ISBN-10: 0-95507-513-0
ISBN-13: 978-0-9550751-3-1

Cover design and typesetting by Reluctant Hero.
www.reluctanthero.co.uk

Printed and bound in the United Kingdom by Mackays of Chatham.

The Custody Minefield is intended for parents separating in England and Wales under the jurisdiction of the English and Welsh Courts. The law referred to in this book is the legislation in force as at August 2006. No liability is accepted for any errors or omissions.

This book does not constitute legal advice and readers should not rely on it as setting out a statement of the law.

ACKNOWLEDGEMENTS

Rob Lewis, Ali Graham, James Brown, Jeremy Cohen, Rufus Harrington, Justine Oldfield-Rowell, Rob and Fran Hall, Peter Davis and Andrew Pawlickzo, Geoff Bowman, Stephen Paul, John and Muriel Dodd, Cathy and David Turner, David Maclean MP, Dr Patrick Gray, Niall Deas, Stephen Deakin, Alistair Orman and the Curry Club Crowd, Melanie and Mark, Sally Kettle.

Ben Bradfield of Orana Publishing for his belief, editorial contribution, and enthusiasm.

My Father, for living the values to which this book aspires.

My Mother, financier, proofreader, cheerleader, campaign manager, friend and saint, who did more than I could ask for, or repay.

CONTENTS

FOREWORD

As a solicitor who has worked with both children and parents for over twenty-five years, and as a father who has had personal experience of the family law system, I would commend this book both to practitioners and to those who become personally involved with issues regarding children (e.g. parents, grandparents, siblings, foster carers). The legal framework designed to regulate and assist parents who cannot agree a regime for their children upon separation is certainly well-meaning, but in reality is constrained by its own shortcomings and uses language that only lawyers understand (or not).

Michael Robinson has managed to put this framework into a language that we can all understand and which helps "de-bunk" the myths that perpetuate the image that most people have – that of "the custody battle". By asking the questions that should be asked at an early stage regarding what are now termed residence issues (i.e. where the children should live) or contact issues (i.e. how often children should see the non-resident parent or extended family), the sting can be taken out of what are inevitably very emotional issues.

When children become embroiled in the already difficult issue of separation, it seems at times that "the system" is either incapable of understanding what you are going through or lacks the sense of urgency that is needed for a resolution. These perfectly understandable feelings cloud your rational thinking and Michael has provided a tool that can be used at any stage in the process to undo muddled thinking.

There is a wealth of information provided which can be used at many levels – as simple as to where to go for professional help, to the much more complex legal and psychological issues that are sometimes involved. I have often heard parents say that "an expert" either "doesn't understand" or "has made his mind up before he saw me", and this book contains practical advice on how to deal with these issues.

It was said to me many years ago that when parents separate there is a rubber ball that they keep throwing to each other. That ball is labelled "R" for Responsibility. I have seen that ball being thrown to the ex-partner who, if they catch it, will become weighed down with someone else's issues that they inevitably cannot understand, while the thrower has "exorcised" themselves of responsibility. To catch the ball leads to emotional dead-end feelings of anger and guilt that are totally non-conducive to resolving conflict in respect of children.

What this book does is to help a parent (or other carer of children) to carry only their own rubber ball and not to throw it to their ex, nor to catch it if is thrown at them. If parents are confused and angry this can only translate to the children. If separating parents can manage to remain focused and flexible, a solution that is understood by their children – and best for them – can usually be found.

This book provides the tools for such a solution. Use it.

Robert Lewis – Solicitor for Children

INTRODUCTION

This book came about following a Sunday barbeque with a group of friends. The topic of conversation turned to the difficulties of agreeing adequate arrangements for children during separation and divorce.

Thousands of parents are missing out on happier agreements. Every year following divorce, up to a fifth of parents lose contact with their children. If they had only known their rights, they may well have been able to secure the chance to maintain this precious relationship with their child. Few applications to the Courts for contact are refused – in fact, less than 1%. Perception of how the Law responds to divorce can be at odds with the modern reality.

So why do parents sometimes fail to achieve the contact and residence agreements they'd prefer with their children? My friends at the barbeque were drawing on a fairly typical range of domestic circumstances. Some had their children living with them, some saw them at weekends, and one had lost contact. All agreed that cost, shortage of time and a lack of information made difficult situations even harder to resolve.

With solicitors frequently charging more than £200 an hour, it was felt that there is often insufficient time to explore fully the options and choices available at the time of separation. Solicitors are often unavailable, and the time that could be spent talking to them is limited by fear of the size of the bill.

Each parent had bought books to inform themselves. Bizarrely, despite the books being published in the United Kingdom, some are written for the American market and of little help since the legislation they refer to clearly doesn't apply on this side of the Atlantic.

Of the titles written for England and Wales, some were unnecessarily pessimistic, failing to take account of gradual changes in the Law and the attitudes of the Courts. Some are biased towards assisting mothers, others on the side of fathers – in both cases missing the vital need to focus on what is best for children. Courts are not interested in the parental or political agendas that these books promote - they are entirely child focused.[1]

None of the friends had found a single book, written for parents, which provided clear, concise, practical and impartial information and which focused on what was best for the children concerned.

We discovered that the Courts consider applications for as many as 125,000 Court Orders each year related to family matters.[2] It was clear that someone had to write a book to help separating parents feel less helpless when navigating their own custody minefield.

This book sets out to cover every potential pitfall that a parent could face from start to finish in a residence or contact Court case. Separation is traumatic enough, but if you also have to deal with domestic violence, mental health problems, false allegations, child abuse or child abduction, your need for information to assist in making informed and objective decisions is even greater.

All the questions which go through our minds in these situations are posed in this book, and answered. In this way your stress and fear, while not being eliminated, can be significantly reduced.

I have deliberately steered away from discussing subjects like "can the relationship be saved?" This book provides you with hard facts on matters that may be outside your experience.

The first section of the book is about mediation, holding to the principle that it's better (and cheaper) to resolve matters without solicitors and the Courts being involved. If you must go to Court, the next sections explain legislation and the Court process, and your options are set out.

There are contact details available at the back of the book for every organisation mentioned, together with explanations of the legal terms that you may come across. As well as an explanation of the law, references are also given to the legal Acts that could affect the reader. My view is that parents should have the means for direct access to legislation.

No matter how hard your case seems, how stressed and tired you feel, remember that your children need you in their lives. Ask for support and help if you need it. Organisations that can provide this are listed in the Useful Contacts section.

Please make use of our website www.thecustodyminefield.com. This provides links to the organisations and most of the legislation referred to in the book. You will also find chat rooms for mothers, fathers, grandparents, and a general community room. There are discussion forums where parents can share ideas, find support and ask one other for advice about parenting matters. We also have anonymous questionnaires about being a contact parent, resident parent, grandparent etc that will help to identify social and legal trends.

Feedback is always welcome so please feel free to send an email with your comments to michael.robinson@thecustodyminefield.com.

I wish you luck, and my thoughts and those of my friends who helped with this book are with you every step of the way.

A last personal piece of advice: if you are fighting your ex-partner purely due to spite, remember the old saying "If you want revenge, dig two graves."

Michael Robinson

1
THE LEGAL PROCESS

Chapter 1 looks at aspects of the legal system relating to Family Law, from mediation to choosing a solicitor, legal aid, how to instruct a solicitor, confidentiality, correspondence, the different types of Court and what to expect in Court.

Simple questions are covered such as:

- "how can I find a solicitor?"

- "what should I call the Judge?"

- "what should I wear?"

There are also answers to more complex matters such as:

- "who can I discuss details of my Court case with?"

- "can I show people a copy of the Court Order?"

- "am I eligible for legal aid?"

The types of Court Order that you can apply for are also mentioned, and are covered in depth in Chapter 2.

1.1 MEDIATION

What is mediation?

'Mediation' is where an independent third party helps parents come to a voluntary agreement about arrangements for their children.

Why should I consider mediation?

Mediation will be cheaper than going to Court. If successful, it stands the greatest chance of an agreement being reached where both parents are happy, and therefore causes less stress for all.

What does a mediator do?

Mediators can assist couples to communicate when they are separating and disagreeing about issues such as financial matters and where their children should live.

Family mediators can give general information about the law and the way the legal system works. They cannot provide advice about a person's legal rights or their best course of action, and can't make decisions for you.

How do I arrange mediation?

You can organise mediation yourself or via your solicitor. Sometimes, a Judge may suggest, or your solicitor may request, that the Court appoint a mediator from the Children and Family Court Advisory and Support Service (CAFCASS). The role of the CAFCASS Officer as a mediator is also discussed in Chapter 4.2.

Which organisations provide mediation services?

Various organisations and individuals provide mediation services. You can find a solicitor specialising in family mediation by contacting the Law Society. You can also contact the UK College of Family Mediators, an organisation that sets standards for family mediation and maintains a register of members who achieve them.

Will I have to pay the mediator?

The service may be free if you are on a low income and you should ask a solicitor if you qualify for legal aid (refer to Chapter 1.3). By reaching an agreement through mediation you could be saved from having to bear the financial (and emotional) costs of a lengthy Court case.

What will happen?

Mediation usually takes between two and four sessions, each lasting about an hour and a half. Mediation only works when both parties voluntarily enter into it.

1.2 CHOOSING LEGAL REPRESENTATION

How do I find the right solicitor?

If your ex-partner won't consider mediation, or if it's been unsuccessful, you will need to choose a solicitor who practices Family Law to represent you in Court.

A good Family Law solicitor will be looking to find areas of agreement and compromise between you and your ex-partner, since the legal profession consider this to be in the best interests of all concerned, particularly the child.

If there are other issues that impact on your situation, such as mental health problems or abuse allegations, ask if the solicitor has specific experience in handling these types of cases. So often, due to the rapid progress of events, people choose the first solicitor they come across.

Consider asking other parents who are separated or divorced if they would recommend their own solicitor (and what the outcome of their case was). Remember, you are paying for the service and are entitled to good service.

The Law Society of England and Wales website has an online service to assist you in finding a solicitor.

Will I need a barrister and what do they do?

Historically, only a barrister was able to act as an advocate for a client in the higher Courts (an advocate in this context being a legally trained professional allowed to speak on your behalf). The solicitor would prepare the client's case and instruct the barrister on their behalf. The law has now been changed allowing solicitors to carry out this role.

Your solicitor may consider instructing (employing) a barrister to assist in your case if specialist legal knowledge is required, and sometimes if there are witnesses or expert witnesses to be cross-examined (questioned in Court). Such a decision should also take into account the additional cost of doing so.

Larger firms of solicitors sometimes have barristers working within their firm (rather than working privately out of a Chambers). Your solicitor will most likely recommend a barrister, but should take account of your personal choice.

What should I ask the solicitor at the first meeting?

Before you meet your solicitor for the first time, consider if it would be better if you approached your ex-partner directly yourself, or whether mediation is a possibility. If you take neither of these to be an option, or are unsure, you could discuss this with the solicitor at the first meeting.

You can also ask the following questions:

- How long will the case take?

- What will the likely costs be?

- Do you qualify for legal aid and if so, does that solicitor do legal aid work (not all solicitors do)?

- What are the chances of success? (Don't expect a definite answer, since other factors such as the Judge who hears the case and the strength of your ex-partner's case will affect the outcome.)

- Could the solicitor help arrange mediation with your ex-partner?

- Could you end up having to pay your ex-partner's legal costs?

- Are they a member of "Resolution first for family law"? This organisation used to be called the Family Law Association and has 5,000 practising family law solicitors as members who follow a code of ethics aimed at constructive, non-confrontational resolution of family law matters.

Was the solicitor right for me?

After the meeting, consider whether the solicitor was able to explain things to you so you understood, how confident they made you feel, and whether they fully understood your situation. Do you think they listened to you? If not, consider seeing a different solicitor.

1.3 FUNDING YOUR COURT CASE

How much will the Court Case cost?

Family law related Court cases are expensive. Depending on the complexity of your case, the unwillingness or inability of your ex-partner to agree to compromise and the need to retain the services of expert witnesses, the cost could be anything from £1,000 to £50,000.

If you qualify for legal aid, the Government covers your legal costs from "the public purse", and this is discussed further on.

If I don't qualify for legal aid, how can I raise money?

You may need to consider a bank loan or help from friends and family in the event that you don't have spare financial resources or assets that can be sold such as investments.

Bear in mind that if you own your home, you may not be able to re-mortgage easily if your home property is in joint names. Consider speaking to a financial advisor to discuss ways of raising funds and managing your finances during the Court case.

How can I reduce my costs?

Being prepared prior to seeing your solicitor, including having your instructions in writing, reduces the amount of time you need to spend in meetings, and saves your solicitor time when preparing your case. This will save you money. Each hour your solicitor spends on your case or talking to you can cost between £150 to £200, sometimes even more.

What is legal aid?

Legal aid is state funded financial assistance used to help people cover some or all of the legal costs associated with separation, including mediation, solicitor's fees, barrister's fees, Court fees, and costs associated with employing expert witnesses.

Can I get legal aid to help me to cover my costs?

To obtain legal aid, you must meet two sets of eligibility criteria, the first based on your financial circumstances, the second based on the merits of your case.

What financial criteria must I meet to be eligible for legal aid?

Financial eligibility is likely to be dependent on your monthly disposable income, gross income, and disposable capital. The main financial criteria are as follows:

- If you are receiving income support, income-based job seeker's allowance, or guarantee state pension credit, you will automatically meet the income and capital criteria.

- If you have four or fewer dependent children, your monthly gross income must not exceed £2,350.

- Your net monthly disposable income must not exceed £649.

- If your net monthly disposable income is between £279 and £649, you will have to make a contribution towards the legal costs as a percentage of your disposable income.

- Your total disposable capital must not exceed £8,000 (disposable capital includes equity in your property, investments, savings etc less any liabilities such as loans, mortgage, and other debts).

- If your disposable capital is more than £3,000, you will have to pay a contribution of either the capital exceeding that sum or the likely maximum funded costs, whichever is less.

  As an example: if you had £3,500 in savings, and your legal fees are £1,500, you would have to contribute £500 towards the costs.

- If you are married or living with someone as a couple, your partner's income will be included in the gross and capital limits unless:

  a) you live apart because your relationship is over

  b) there is a conflict of interest between you (for example you want advice about a divorce).

For more detailed eligibility criteria including assistance in working out your net disposable income and total disposable capital, speak to a solicitor or refer to the Legal Services Commission.[3]

Figures provided in this chapter are provided as an indication of the financial eligibility criteria as at April 2006 and may be subject to change, and you are advised to confirm independently whether the merits of your case and financial circumstances allow you to qualify.

Will I have to pay the legal aid money back?

If your Court case includes settling financial matters and the recovery of money or property (which may be the case in a divorce settlement or the division of assets following separation for an unmarried couple), your solicitor may use these funds to pay his or her bill. There are some exceptions to this, including if the money or property recovered consists of maintenance payments.

Is there special help for people experiencing domestic violence?

There are special rules relating to legal funding for cases involving domestic violence (cases where some form of protection for the individual is involved). You can find details of the criteria relating to domestic violence by contacting the Legal Services Commission.

Do all solicitors do legal aid work?

No. The Legal Services Commission (LSC) is the body responsible for looking after legal aid in England and Wales. Solicitors must hold a contract with the LSC before they can do legal aid work.

How do I find a solicitor who is contracted to do legal aid work?

You can contact the LSC to find a solicitor who is contracted with them to provide legal aid.

1.4 INSTRUCTING A SOLICITOR

What is a solicitor's role?

A solicitor is there to represent your wishes, explain to the Court what you want to see happen, give your history of events, and ask the Court to consider making a decision in your favour. They help you by filling in the right paperwork, putting together your statement for the Court, and then managing your case while it goes through the legal process.

Family Law solicitors help to try to resolve matters amicably, and will most likely attempt to do this via correspondence with your ex-partner or more likely his or her solicitor, if one has been employed.

Solicitors provide you with choices and then assist you with your chosen course of action. Solicitors only know what you tell them and take instruction from you about what you want to do. They should listen to what you have to say, and then advise you what actions are open to you through the legal system.

What should I do in preparation for my first meeting with them?

Before your first meeting, try to prepare the following to help your solicitor:

1. **Outcome:** Write down an outline of what would be the ideal Court decision or outcome. Consider what is best for your children, not for you, since this is what the Court will do. Next consider the "worst" situation you could accept and also where you'd be prepared to compromise.

2. **History:** Write a chronology (diary) setting out a history of events (including dates and times if you can) leading up to your decision to go to Court. Let your solicitor decide what is relevant and what isn't. Remember the solicitor will only know what you tell them.

3. **Concerns:** Note down any concerns you have about your ex-partner's circumstances or ability to care for your children. If you don't have any but think you are more suitable to be their main carer, that's fine. The Court won't appreciate unfounded allegations, and any allegations you make are likely to be tested in Court to see if they are valid.

4. **Contact:** If you're not applying to be your child's main carer (have your child primarily reside with you), but simply to ensure you see your child regularly, then what does "regularly" mean to you?

   If you're not currently seeing your child at all then as a matter of urgency have your solicitor approach the Court to request they make an immediate Interim Contact Order (this is a temporary order until the Final Hearing lays down what will happen in the long term).

   It is important for both you and your child that your relationship is maintained while the Court case progresses (which can take months).

   Again, give thought as to whether this would be every weekend with you, every other weekend, times during the week so you can be involved with school, as well as how much of their holidays they would spend with you.

Think of the practicalities of the arrangements including how you can balance looking after your child with work commitments. Can you carry on your current job and look after your child at the same time and to the same standard (or better) that your ex-partner can?

5. **Consider Joint Residence:** This means both parents have an equal status in bringing up their child (although the child may spend more time with one or other parent). A letter from your solicitor to your ex-partner suggesting this, and looking at mediation to agree the amount of time the child spends with each parent, is likely to be best for the child due to less conflict. This will save a great deal of expense, and you will be demonstrating your maturity in accepting your ex-partner's importance in your child's life.

6. **Confirm whether you have legal Parental Responsibility:** It is vital to ensure that you have legal Parental Responsibility (refer to Chapter 3.1 which explains why and whether you have it). If not, discuss this with your solicitor as a priority.

7. **Risks and Fast Action:** If you think your partner could be a risk to your child due to mental health problems, drug or alcohol dependency, or other identified risks, then act quickly. Talk to your solicitor about the possibility of an Emergency Protection Order and a Recovery Order. See also the Chapters on Social Services and Mental Health.

Don't rely on others to protect your children. They are your responsibility and Government agencies have been known to make mistakes. If you have concerns about your ex-partner, try to assemble evidence to support your case for the first meeting.

Again remember that the Court won't view you positively if you make unfounded allegations. Don't appear malicious, no matter what unpleasantness has occurred in the past.

8. **Allegations:** If you expect your partner to make allegations, then alert your solicitor. The more prepared your legal team, the less chance of them being caught without a response, rebuttal or explanation.

If you are making allegations, how will you present those fairly, or defend yourself against counter-allegations from your ex-partner? Don't go to Court on the premise that you are innocent until proven guilty.

Family Courts make a decision on the lowest level of evidence. This is known as the "balance of probability": in essence, what seems most likely, or will limit risks. They will take allegations of domestic violence and abuse extremely seriously, and rightfully so, and while these are being investigated, may reduce or stop your contact with your child.

You could find yourself waiting months before these investigations are concluded, and during that time, your ex-partner will have been the main carer for your child, and the Courts may be unwilling to change the situation as the child is now used to living with them.

9. **Evidence:** If you face allegations of parental unfitness, or have these concerns about your partner, what evidence is there to support this or defend against it?

Depending on your child's age, consider asking for statements from the Health Visitor, Play Group, or refer to their school records. Medical reports, psychologist's reports and counselling reports could all help, but your solicitor may need the Court to make an order to obtain these if they relate to your ex-partner. Statements in support of your parenting ability will help.

If Social Services have previously carried out assessments due to concerns about your child's welfare, you are entitled to a copy of their reports.[4]

If your ex-partner has been at home looking after the child and you have been the main earner, or vice versa, the Court will be unlikely to want to change this situation, without very good cause.

10. **How would you care for your child if the Court granted you residence?** Think how you would look after your child. Would it require a change in job, use of child minders or help from grandparents? How would you financially support your child AND look after them? Compare your situation to your ex-partner's and consider what would cause the child the least disruption.

11. **Your Finances:** If you need legal aid, be ready to discuss details of the equity you have in your home, your gross earnings, and your monthly disposable income. The criteria for qualifying for legal aid can change, and you may need to provide your solicitor with additional information before they can confirm whether you qualify for free or subsidised legal assistance.

12. **Your Future:** What is the best outcome for you, as well as your child? Have you considered what being a single parent means?

You may find that having the child stay with your ex-partner for a weekend, every other week, gives you the opportunity for a social life, some romance in your life, time for hobbies, or even the occasional lie-in.

13. **The Welfare Checklist:** Ensure your own application takes the Welfare Checklist into consideration (since the Court will), and consider the merits of your ex-partner's case in relation to this (refer to Chapter 2.1).

Consider what your solicitor says and any advice they give, but remember that the decision is yours alone, and that you will need to live with what happens at the end of the Court case while your solicitor will move onto the next case.

1.5 PREPARING FOR COURT

What do I need to do before going to Court?

You need to decide which type of Court Order to apply for, and have your solicitor make a formal application to the Court for a Judge to consider granting your request. An 'order' in this context is a written decision of the Court.

Can I apply for a Court Order if my child is over the age of sixteen?

No. The Children Act 1989 states that the Court Orders described in this chapter may only be made in exceptional circumstances for children over the age of sixteen.[5]

How do I inform the Court of the events which led to my decision to go to Court, and what I want to happen?

You do this by writing a statement for the Court, and your solicitor will help you structure it in the right way.

Be clear about your reasons for wanting the order, ensure the reasons stay focussed on what your children need, and don't include petty issues. Support your statement and the application for the order with as much evidence you can.

If you partner has problems that have an adverse affect on your children then you should list these and explain how your partner's behaviour affects them.

Bear in mind that due to time limits your solicitor may not get the opportunity to present all of your evidence before a Final Hearing, so consider including as much information in your statement as you can.

What type of Court Order should I choose?

Different Court Orders address different situations, and the type of Court Order(s) you apply for will depend on your circumstances, and what you want to happen.

You can apply for the following Court Orders:[6]

- **Contact Orders** set down how much contact the child has with the parent they don't live with (the non-resident parent) and how the contact will take place.

- **Residence Orders** favour a single parent being the primary carer and the children having their main home with that parent. Residence is the modern term for custody.

- **Joint (or shared) Residence Orders** set down that regardless of the amount of time the child lives with each parent, essentially the children have two homes and both parents have equal rights.

- **Emergency Protection Orders** can be made where a Judge considers that the children are at risk of 'significant harm'. This type of order is intended to temporarily remove the children to a place of safety while allegations are investigated, or remove the person accused of causing the harm from their home.

- **Recovery Orders** are used to return children to the person who makes the application. This type of order can be made to enable the return of children when a Residence Order is broken, or to set out the way in which the children are recovered if an Emergency Protection Order has been made.

- **Prohibited Steps Orders** limit the involvement of a parent in making decisions and taking actions that affect their children. A Prohibited Steps Order could be used to prevent a parent from refusing medical treatment for their child, if it was felt that such refusal would be harmful to the child.

- **Specific Issue Orders** address areas of disagreement between parents. This form of order could be used to set out where the children go to school if parents disagree.

What happens next?

Normally, both you and your ex-partner will be contacted with a date to attend a First Hearing.

Your solicitor will send a copy of your statement to your ex-partner or their solicitor, and your ex-partner will most likely write their own statement for the Court to consider. Your and your ex-partner's statement must include the substance of any oral evidence that you intend to present to the Court.

If you intend to present evidence to the Court that supports your case, your ex-partner will be entitled to see a copy of it first to allow them to prepare their own case.[7]

Will my ex-partner always be informed of the Court case and invited to attend?

Your ex-partner will normally be invited to attend. Exceptions can occur in circumstances where your ex-partner has simply disappeared and every effort has been made to contact them, or where the children are considered to be at risk and you are applying to the Court for an Emergency Protection Order. A hearing without the other party present is called an ex-parte hearing.

Following an ex-parte hearing, and any subsequent Court Orders made, your ex-partner will have the right to challenge the Court's decision at a future hearing.

A hearing with both parties present is called an inter-parte hearing.

1.6 DIFFERENT COURTS AND COURT ETIQUETTE

What type of Court will hear the case?

Your case could be dealt with in either:

- the Magistrates Court (also known as the Family Proceedings Court)
- the Crown Court
- the High Court

If your case is relatively simple and does not include divorce (but only what happens to your children), it is more likely to be heard by the Family Proceedings Court. For more complex cases or where contact/residence is involved as a part of divorce proceedings, the matter is likely to be heard by the Crown Court. It may be decided that due to the complexity of the case, the case should be heard in the High Court.

What type of Judge will hear the case?

The type of Judge depends on the type of Court your case is heard in:

- A Magistrates Court is presided over by either a Magistrate or a District Judge.
- A Crown Court is presided over by either a District Judge or a Crown Court Judge.
- The High Court is presided over by a High Court Judge.

How should I address the Judge?

Etiquette is important in Court, and different Judges are addressed in different ways:

- Magistrates should be called Sir, Madam or Your Worship.
- District Judges should be called Sir, Madam or Judge.
- County Court Judges should be called Your Honour.
- High Court Judges should be called Your Worship.

Do my ex-partner and I have formal titles?

Yes. If you are the person who makes the application to the Court, you're referred to as the 'Applicant', while the other party (your ex-partner) is known as the 'Respondent'. The parent with whom the children live may also be referred to as the 'resident parent' while the other parent may be called 'non-resident parent'.

Who else will be in the Courtroom?

Family law cases are private, so aside from yourself, your ex-partner, your solicitors (and barristers if you're using them), the other two people in the Courtroom will be the Judge and the Clerk.

What does the Clerk do?

The Clerk is the person who fetches you and takes you into the Courtroom. They will ask you to stand when the Judge enters the Court, and will be present during the hearing. If you are representing yourself, you will need to tell a Clerk when you arrive at the Court building, and also hand them any paperwork that the Judge needs to see before the hearing starts. If you have a solicitor, they will do this for you. The Clerk may ask you to swear an oath before you give verbal evidence.

What will the Courtroom be like and what will people wear?

The Family Proceedings Court is more informal than a criminal Court, so expect a large table with all parties seated round it, including your own and your ex-partner's solicitors and the Magistrate or District Judge.

At a Family Proceedings Court (Magistrates Court), it is normal for everyone to be dressed smartly. No one will be wearing robes or wigs.

The County Court is more formal. It is possible that the District Judge or County Court Judge will speak to you in the same Courtroom used for criminal cases. The Judge will sit higher, and you will sit with your solicitor and barrister (who may sit in front of you), and the same will apply to your ex-partner and their legal team.

Again, family law cases are more informal, so wigs won't be worn, although the Judge may wear a robe.

How should I behave in Court?

In Court, protocol and tradition are still important, as is showing the Court respect. Stand when the Judge enters the room and keep quiet unless asked to contribute something by your solicitor or the Judge. If you think your solicitor has missed something, tap them on the shoulder and pass them a note to bring your concern to their attention. It is worth taking a pad in with you, and copies of ALL relevant documentation for reference purposes.

What will the Judge be like?

Most Judges are understanding and work hard at being fair. It is difficult for anyone walking into Court and seeing their ex-partner in this type of situation. Going into Court isn't as frightening as you imagine and your solicitor is there to help you. The Judge will be aware of how hard this is for you and act accordingly.

1.7 THE COURT CASE

What happens when I walk into the Court building?

Your solicitor may have asked you to arrive early to give you both time to discuss any last minute preparations, to confirm your instructions or see if you have had any change of thought about your case. There are meeting rooms available to allow for private discussion.

You may find that despite your case being set for a certain time, it gets delayed. Cases can overrun, and several cases may be scheduled for the same day, since the Court has to deal with cases being cancelled due to parents reaching agreement between themselves, or witnesses or parties to the proceedings failing to show up or being late.

Your solicitor will inform the Clerk that you have arrived in Court, and the Clerk will come and tell you when the Judge is ready to hear your case.

What will happen when I go to Court?

The first time you go to Court, this will be for an Initial Hearing. Initial Hearings are often short in length (sometimes only half an hour). The Judge will have read the statements from the two parties, and have considered what you both have asked to happen.

At this hearing the Judge may call for expert witnesses to provide an opinion on the family's circumstances by asking Social Services or CAFCASS to carry out investigations and provide independent reports.

Other parties may be called on for information such as your child's school,

General Practitioner or Health Visitor. The Court may wish both parties to try mediation if you and your ex-partner haven't already done so.

How many hearings will there be?

If the Court requests that investigations be carried out, it is possible that there will be further Interim Hearings before the Judge has sufficient information to make a final decision at the Final Hearing. These Interim Hearings will either be 'directions hearings' to ask for additional investigations to be carried out, or 'finding of fact hearings' to hear the reports and opinion of the experts who carried out the investigation.

Once all investigations have been concluded and expert reports filed and examined, a date for a Final Hearing will be set. At the Final Hearing both you and your ex-partner will have the opportunity to challenge or agree with the experts' reports, cross-examine witnesses, and to have your legal representative present your final argument.

Any hearing can become a Final Hearing if both you and your ex-partner reach an agreement, after which the Judge may then formalise the arrangements to which you have agreed.

Will any decisions be made before the Final Hearing?

If delays are expected, the Judge may decide to make an interim order, essentially a temporary order setting out how things will be until such time as the parents reach agreement, or investigations have been concluded and their findings considered by the Judge (whichever comes first).

What kind of interim order could be made?

The Judge may decide to make an interim order granting temporary residence to one parent, and formalising contact arrangements between the other parent and the children. It is likely that the Judge will encourage both parents to reach agreement for the "interim period" before the next or Final Hearing. The willingness of the parties to keep to temporary agreements will be noted by the Court.

How long with the Court case take?

In an ideal world Court cases involving children would be dealt with quickly, although in reality this isn't the case. Frustrating as this is, there are a number of good reasons:

- When setting a hearing date, the Court has to have a spare time "slot".
- The required investigations and assessments can take time.
- Both legal teams have to be available on that date.
- Experts or other witnesses must be available on that day.
- If any of the above are ill, the case may be adjourned (set for another date).
- Sometimes the Court and legal representatives (solicitors and barristers) double-book because it isn't unusual for parents to reach compromise and for a hearing then to become unnecessary.
- Sometimes other cases overrun.
- In practice, family law cases often take many months and delays can happen for many reasons. Be prepared for this.

What is the Court's responsibility regarding the time investigations take?

Investigations are undertaken when parents have two very different histories of events and opinions about the child's current circumstances. One parent may have concerns about the other's ability to care for the child, and there may be fears for the child's safety. While the Judge won't want unnecessary delays, investigation will help the Judge make an informed decision.

The Judge will order that, when an investigation is required to answer specific questions raised in Court, it should be concluded within a specified timescale. The Judge will draw up a timetable for expert witnesses and the parties to the proceedings (yourself, your ex-partner, and your legal representatives) to work to.[8] The Judge will also set out the steps required to help ensure that the investigations are successfully concluded within the desired timescale.

Will the Judge only make an order if there is clear evidence support?

The Judge will generally grant an order in favour of whoever appears most plausible (according to what is called the "balance of probability"), not on the basis of firm and conclusive evidence. They will only make an order if they consider it to be necessary and in the child's best interests.

The more evidence you provide, the stronger your case. If your ex-partner doesn't have proof, that doesn't mean they won't be believed. Prepare for this possibility by building up a solid defence against allegations if they are made, and be pro-active.

What do Judges base their decisions on?

In terms of considering whether to make an order, and which type of order to make, the Judge will base the decision foremost on the principles set out in the Welfare Checklist (refer to Chapter 2.1) and how they relate to the child's and parents' circumstances.

When preparing your case, you must ensure that your application is built upon these principles.

Regardless of how your ex-partner has behaved towards you, if your child's interests are best served by primarily residing with your ex-partner, the Court will consider the welfare of the children first and foremost. Even if you were the one who applied to the Court, the Judge may rule in your ex-partner's favour.

What decision will the Court make ?

While you may approach the Court wanting one type of order, the Court can impose any order that it sees fit for a child under the age of 16, once having heard your evidence, evidence from third parties (if they become involved), and evidence from your ex-partner.

The decision about your child's future, once the matter goes to Court, won't be made by you or your ex-partner, unless you reach an agreement before the end of the Final Hearing. The Children Act 1989 encourages you to do this with something it calls the "no order principle", where if the parents have reached agreement, the Court will make "no order" unless the Judge believes that making an order is in the child's best interests (and they need a good reason for this).

It is important to be aware that in circumstances where one parent has been the primary carer for their children while the other parent worked, it is unlikely that the Court will agree to a change in this situation without very good reason.

The Court holds the opinion that a change in circumstances can be harmful to children and that in most circumstances maintaining the status quo is in the child's best interests. If your children are living with your ex-partner while the Court case progresses, delays can strengthen the likelihood of their gaining residence due to the status quo principle.[9]

1.8 TIPS FOR COURT ATTENDANCE

- **Do clear out your pockets or handbag before leaving home.** Courts usually have metal detectors, and security staff will search your bags when you enter the building. Take in only what you need.

- **Don't be late.** Allow time for traffic jams, finding parking places, missed buses, or cancelled trains.

- **Do dress smartly** (Judges like to be shown respect).

- **Do take an umbrella.** It sounds obvious, but there is nothing worse than turning up in Court dripping wet. Also ensure any paperwork you take with you is in something waterproof.

- **Do take a coat or a jumper.** Some Courts can be baking hot (especially the rooms set aside for you to talk to your solicitor) and the corridors can be cold depending on the age of the Court building.

- **Do use Court delay time:** If the hearing is delayed, and you find yourself at one end of a corridor with your solicitor, with your ex-partner at the other end with theirs, don't waste this time (you're paying for it) – negotiate! See if a compromise can be reached. Set your solicitor running up and down the corridor (they're used to it).

- **Don't stare out your ex-partner.**

- **Don't ever interrupt the Judge.**

- **Don't get angry – stay calm.**

- **Do take a pad and pen into the Court.** Make notes, and if you need to say something to your solicitor, write it down and hand it across to them (or a note saying "I need to speak to you about this"). The Judge is usually quite observant and will point out to the solicitor that "your client wishes to speak to you" and allow you some time.

- **Do follow your solicitor's advice in Court.**
- **Don't make plans for the rest of the day.** You could be tied up for hours.
- **Do make contingency plans** in case you are tied up in Court for hours (make arrangements for the children to be picked up, and have enough cash on you for the parking meter).
- **Do take a drink and some food and something to read.**
- **Do turn off your mobile phone** before you walk into the Court room.

1.9 CONFIDENTIALITY IN COURT

Who can I talk to about the Court Case?

Details of your Court case must be treated in confidence, although you are allowed to share information and discuss them with: [10]

- your solicitor or barrister.
- any other parties in your case.
- a CAFCASS Officer, Welsh Family Proceedings Officer or a Welfare Officer.
- the Legal Services Commission.
- an expert authorised by the Court.
- a professional, including the Police and the NSPCC, whose job it is to protect children.
- a lay adviser (e.g. Citizens Advice Bureau) or a McKenzie friend (person granted permission by the Court to assist you and give advice, take notes etc), to allow you to get help and advice in connection with your case and in Court.
- your spouse, cohabitant or close family member, so you can have confidential discussions with them.
- a health care professional or a person/body providing counselling services for children and families, so you can seek health care or counselling for you or your child.
- the Children's Commissioner or the Children's Commissioner for Wales, so you can refer a matter to them which may affect the interests of children.
- a person or body conducting an approved research project, so that they can carry out the project.

- a mediator so that you can receive mediation in relation to the proceedings.
- a person or body responsible for investigating complaints about legal representatives or advisers so that they can investigate or determine the complaint in question.

With whom am I allowed to discuss details of the Court Orders?

In addition to the individuals and organisations mentioned above, you can discuss the text of a Court Order with:[10]

- your Member of Parliament (MP), Member of European Parliament elected in England and Wales, National Assembly Member, or a Member of the House of Lords so they can advise you, investigate a complaint or raise a question related to policy or procedure.
- the General Medical Council so you can make a complaint to the GMC.
- a Police Officer so they can investigate a crime, or whether a crime has been committed.
- a member of the Crown Prosecution Service so that it can carry out its legal functions.

If there are other people who you feel should be aware of details of a Court Order, such as your child's school or General Practitioner, you need to ask the Court for permission before you can do this. Your solicitor can help you to do this.

What could happen if I talk to someone who isn't on this list?

Unless you have the permission of the Court, sharing information with an unauthorised person, or publishing details of your Court case publicly or within the media, can be a 'Contempt of Court'.[11]

How should I share information about the case or Court Order?

If you do need to share information (within the restrictions detailed in this Chapter) ensure anything in writing includes the wording "Private and Confidential" and that the people you either tell or give the information to are aware of the restrictions. Keep a record of the people you handed information to, and the reason why you did.

Do my solicitor and barrister have to treat what I tell them in confidence?

Yes, although solicitors and barristers also have a duty not to mislead the Court. If they become aware of information that is harmful to your case and you withhold your permission for them to disclose it to the Court, they are entitled to refuse to continue to work for you.

Are there circumstances in which a solicitor will break their duty of confidentiality to me?

Yes. A solicitor should consider breaking the confidentiality rule in circumstances where they consider there to be serious health risks to a child or a threat to a child's life.

1.10 CORRESPONDENCE

There are some general tips to share regarding correspondence:

- Put together a simple filing system. It is likely that the Court case will generate volumes of paperwork. Have a system that ensures you can find paperwork quickly and don't lose it.

- If the letters you send are important, either hand deliver them or send them by registered post so that you have proof of dispatch.

- Keep a copy of all letters you send and receive. Make a note of when and to whom you delivered them personally, or keep the recorded delivery slip with the photocopy.

- Keep a printed copy of any emails you send.

- Ensure your solicitor has copies of all of your important paperwork.

- If you keep your letters on your computer, keep a separate backup copy.

- Ask for, and keep a copy of, all reports, statements and Court Orders.[7]

- Your solicitor will prepare your statements to the Court on your behalf, ensuring that they are based on what you say, but phrased in the correct way, and complying with the correct format. As this is your statement, ask to read it before it is sent to the Court and your ex-partner's solicitor. Mistakes can be made, especially since solicitors rarely do their own typing. The statement sets out your argument, and puts in a written form the substance of what you intend to say in Court.

- You may wish to check any letters before they are sent out on your behalf by your solicitor. This can be done by having your solicitor fax or email you a copy before they post the letter. There is a cost for doing this so use your discretion.

- Your solicitor will be handling many cases, you will be absorbed by only one. You may need to chase your solicitor but, regardless, ask to be kept informed of what is happening, and if things seem to be delayed, ask why. Push them if you need to.

- Make friends with your solicitor's secretary. They will be the person that you deal with when your solicitor is unavailable.

- Ensure your solicitor keeps you regularly informed of how much you owe them and what the likely costs will be.

- Try not to have your solicitor send letters to your ex-partner for frivolous reasons. These costs can quickly multiply.

2

THE WELFARE CHECKLIST AND COURT ORDERS

In Chapter 2 we look at the Welfare Checklist and the Court Orders that you could apply for, or that the Court may see fit to make, depending on your circumstances.

The Welfare Checklist is the set of principles set out in the Children Act 1989 which the Court must consider when determining what judgment it should make in relation to cases involving children. If CAFCASS become involved in assessing your family circumstances and who is best able to look after your children, they will also base their investigation and recommendations on these.

It is incredibly important that your case and your reasons for going to Court adhere to the principles of the Welfare Checklist, and that you consider how these principles relate to your ex-partner's circumstances.

If you can't reach agreement with your ex-partner, you can apply for a number of different Court Orders. This may simply be to ensure you have contact with your children (Contact Order), to have them live with you while you act as their main carer (Residence Order), or ideally to share the upbringing of your children equally with your ex-partner (Joint Residence Order).

If you consider your children are at risk of 'significant harm' in your ex-partner's care, you could consider an Emergency Protection Order and Recovery Order to have your child returned to you while an investigation into the allegations is carried out. Social Services are automatically informed when the Court makes these orders.

If there are matters concerning your children's upbringing that you can't agree on, you can apply to the Courts for a Specific Issue Order and ask the Court to make the decision. If you believe that your ex-partner should be prevented from making certain decisions about your children's upbringing, you could apply for a Prohibited Steps Order.

In exceptional circumstances, the Court can also consider making a Family Assistance Order to provide help during the separation, and to ensure there is support for the children and parents.

Being the person who brings the case to Court (the Applicant) does not mean the Court will rule in your favour unless it considers that your circumstances and reason for the application best conform to the principles set out in the Welfare Checklist.

2.1 THE WELFARE CHECKLIST

What is the Welfare Checklist?

The Welfare Checklist is a list of principles that both a Judge and a CAFCASS Officer must consider when assessing cases that involve children. These principles include consideration of: [12]

(a)　the ascertainable wishes and feelings of the child concerned (considered in the light of his age and understanding);

(b)　his physical, emotional and educational needs;

(c)　the likely effect on him of any change in his circumstances;

(d)　his age, sex, background and any characteristics of his which the court considers relevant;

(e)　any harm which he has suffered or is at risk of suffering;

(f)　how capable each of his parents, and any other person in relation to whom the court considers the question to be relevant, is of meeting his needs;

(g)　the range of powers available to the court under this Act in the proceedings in question.

© Crown Copyright 1989

How are the principles applied?

The Welfare Checklist is deliberately open to interpretation and not prescriptive, as the Court considers that every child's circumstances and needs may be different. Due to this ambiguity, it isn't possible to give precise guidance. For example, it isn't possible to say what age a child should be to have sufficient understanding of the implications of their views to be taken into account. Children of the same age can be at different stages of development.

Hypothetical examples of how the checklist may apply are as follows:

- If your child had a disability and you had a background working with children with special needs, this would count in your favour, in terms of benefit to both your child's physical needs, and their development.
- During residence proceedings, if your ex-partner made it known they intended to move to another city, this would count against them. The children would suffer disruption, both in terms of a move to a new school, and in terms of reduced contact with yourself, their friends and grandparents.
- A parent having a history of drug addiction or alcoholism may be considered less suitable to provide care than a parent without these problems.

None of these examples would guarantee which parent would be granted a Residence Order. A Judge will consider the family circumstances in their entirety, but each principle in the Welfare Checklist has importance in helping them make their decision.

How does the Court find out what my children want to happen?

Where the wishes and the feelings of your children are to be taken into account, it is most likely that a CAFCASS investigation will be requested by the Court, and that the CAFCASS Officer will meet with the children to discuss their wishes with them. The Court will only look at including your children's wishes if they consider them to be old enough to understand the implications of their opinions.

2.2 CONTACT ORDER

What is a Contact Order?

A Contact Order places responsibility on the resident parent to provide the child for contact for the periods of time set out in the Contact Order.[13]

Who can apply for a Contact Order?

Any parent or guardian of the children can apply for a Contact Order.[14]

Are the Courts likely to refuse an application for a Contact Order?

No. In practice, less than 1% of applications to the Court for Contact Orders are refused.[15]

What are the different types of contact that can be specified in a Court Order?

There are two types of contact, direct and indirect. Direct contact includes staying contact (overnight), visiting contact or supervised contact (in a contact centre or with a third party present). Indirect contact includes contact by phone and via correspondence.

Will the Contact Order specify the times that the children see me?

Not necessarily. Contact Orders can be general, in terms of just reminding the resident parent of their responsibility to "make the child available for contact", or specific, to the extent of specifying dates and times that you can see your children.

When are Contact Orders usually made?

The Court will consider making a Contact Order when parents are unable to agree on either the principle of contact, or the practical arrangements and times for contact to take place.

As a non-resident (contact) parent, is there anything else that I should be aware of?

Yes. If there is a Residence Order in force, you cannot take your children abroad or change their names unless you have the Court's permission or the permission of each person with parental responsibility for the children.[16]

If you plan to take your children on holidays abroad, and believe your ex-partner may not agree to your doing so, have your solicitor ask the Judge to give you permission in order to prevent the expense and inconvenience of a return to Court in the future.

I want to be the Resident Parent, why do I need to know about Contact Orders?

If your children are living with your ex-partner while you apply for Residence, and you are unhappy with the amount of contact you have with your children during this time, you could consider asking the Court to make an interim Contact Order. This ensures you see them regularly in the time leading up to the Final Hearing.

If you are the resident parent, you can also apply to the Court for a Contact Order to regulate the amount and nature of contact that your children have with your ex-partner.

Does the non-resident parent have to see their children if they are named in a Contact Order?

No. A Contact Order doesn't compel a non-resident parent to see their children, but places a responsibility on the resident parent to make the children available.

Who else can apply for a Contact Order?

People who meet any of the following criteria also have the automatic right to apply for contact with your children:[17]

1. Any party to a marriage where the children were a part of their family.
2. If they lived with the children for at least three years within the last five years, and their application to the Court is made within three months of the children no longer living with them.[18]
3. If there is a Residence Order in force, and they have the consent of the person with whom the children legally reside.
4. If the children are in Local Authority care and they have the consent of the Local Authority.
5. If they have the consent of each person who holds Parental Responsibility for the children.

For people who don't meet these criteria, when reaching the decision to grant permission, the Court will consider the merits of their application, their connection with your children and whether granting a Contact Order would cause harm to the children.[19]

It is worth noting that your children could also ask the Court's permission to make a Contact Order although the Court must be satisfied that they have sufficient understanding to make such a request.[20]

2.3 RESIDENCE ORDER

What is a Residence Order?

A Residence Order (this used to be called a Custody Order) settles the arrangements for where your children will live.[13]

Along with a Residence Order, the Court may make a Contact Order specifying the amount of contact the non-resident parent should have in the event that the Court considers this necessary (if the resident parent doesn't appear to accept the principles and practicality of a voluntary contact arrangement).

Can I apply for a Residence Order ?

Any parent or guardian of the children can apply for a Residence Order.[14]

Do the Courts more commonly grant the Mother residence of the children?

It is very much dependent on the circumstances of both parents. There is nothing written in law showing bias to either mother or father, although in practice the mother is more usually granted residence. This is often due to the following circumstances:

- the mother has been main carer for the children during the relationship

- the status quo principle (the current circumstances) being that the children may currently reside with the mother (in which case, if the situation is working for the children, the Court will be reluctant to change it)

- historically it was felt that mothers were more suitable carers for young children, although more recent evidence suggests that either parent can fulfill this role. Since the 1990s there has been a growing acceptance of the "house husband"

- the financial welfare of the children is a factor in considering where the children should live. Historically the father has been the main earner or financial contributor to the household. This has now changed.

When does a Residence Order end?

As with other Orders relating to children, when the children reach the age of 16. Additionally, a Residence Order is no longer valid if the parents reconcile and have been living together for six months or more.[21]

If one parent has 'residence', does the other still have a right to involvement in decisions which affect their children?

Possibly. A parent's right to involvement in decisions such as schooling and medical treatment is a separate matter, and depends on their having legal 'Parental Responsibility' (see Chapter 3).

If I'm granted residence, does this place any restrictions on what I can do with my children?

Yes. If you are the resident parent, you cannot take your children abroad for more than one month or change their names without the permission of the Court or the agreement of all parties who have Parental Responsibility for the children.[22]

Can people other than parents apply for a Residence Order?

Yes. People who meet any of the following criteria have the automatic right to apply for residence in relation to your children (without the need to ask the Court's permission to apply first):[17]

1. Any party to a marriage where the children were a part of their family.
2. If they lived with the children for at least three years within the last five years, and their application to the Court is made within three months of the children no longer living with them.[18]
3. If there is a Residence Order in force, and they have the consent of the person with whom the children legally reside.
4. If the children are in Local Authority care and they have the consent of the Local Authority.
5. If they have the consent of each person who holds Parental Responsibility for the children.

For people who don't meet these criteria, when reaching the decision to grant permission, the Court will consider the merits of their application, their connection with your children and whether granting a Residence Order would cause harm to the children.[19]

It is worth noting that your children could also ask the Court's permission to apply for a Residence Order although the Court must be satisfied that they have sufficient understanding to make such a request.[20]

2.4 JOINT RESIDENCE ORDER

What is a Joint Residence Order?

A Joint Residence Order is a Residence Order made in favour of both parents. This type of order grants the parents equal rights in the upbringing of their children.

The Order may specify the practical arrangements for the time the children spend living with each parent.

Will the children live half the time with me?

It's unlikely this will happen. The amount of time children spend with each parent may be no different than if there was a Residence Order in favour of one parent, and a Contact Order in favour of the other.

What is the difference between a Residence and Contact Order, and a Joint Residence Order?

Were a Residence and Contact Order in place, and the resident parent to die, the non-resident parent would need to apply for a Residence Order to have their children live with them. With Joint Residence, if one parent dies, the children already have a home with the other parent.

With the children grieving, they wouldn't have to worry about who was going to look after them. For this reason alone, both parents should consider Joint Residence Orders as being in the best interest of their children.

A Joint Residence Order removes the perception by the parent who spends less time with the children that they can only see their children with the Court's permission (which a Contact Order can imply).

A further important difference, in terms of parental equality, is that neither parent needs the permission of the other to take the children abroad for periods of up to one month.[23]

Are there any other benefits to this type of Order?

Yes. If you are applying for residence of your child, an application for Joint Residence shows your respect for your ex-partner as a parent, and acknowledges their importance in your child's life. This demonstrates not only that you are acting in your child's best interests, but may cause less hostility with your ex-partner than applying for a Residence Order. However, the time that the children spend with each parent will still need to be agreed.

There may be financial benefits for the family if you have more than one child. Joint Residence potentially allows both parents to claim additional personal tax allowance (and possibly one parent benefits, family credit, and additional child benefit). This can be achieved by allowing both parents to claim that one of their children lives with them and thus be entitled to benefits. Non-resident parents can't make this claim.

I've heard Joint Residence Orders are rare, is this true?

Yes, although this is changing.

Unlike other forms of Court Order, such as Contact Orders and Residence Orders, there has been confusion within the judiciary and changes of opinion of when a Court should consider a Joint Residence Order since the legislation was originally made.

There are several reasons for this. Initial guidance for the Court published in 1991 suggested Joint Residence Orders only be made in exceptional circumstances because children needed the stability of single home. The guidance did however go on to state that where children spend considerable time with both parents it was a "more realistic" form of Order than a Residence Order in favour of one parent alone.[24]

There was also a belief that Joint Residence Orders could only work when parents were in agreement. This was the principle reason why few Joint Residence Orders were made, since where parents were in agreement the Court wouldn't feel the need to make an order (the "no order principle" would apply).

Another misconception was that Joint Residence meant that the children would spend equal time living with each parent.

Has the opinion of the Court changed?

Yes, although sole Residence Orders are more common as some misconceptions remain.

For this reason, if you intend to apply for Joint Residence, it is worthwhile being aware of cases where these misconceptions were addressed by the High Court. These cases can, to some extent, be used to demonstrate legal precedent, considering the seniority of the Judges involved.

As early as 1994, the President of the Family Court Division stated that the prevailing view that Joint Residence Orders could only be made in exceptional circumstances "was still too restrictive".[25]

In a case heard in the Court of Appeal in 2001 it was stated that the residency of the children could be shared, even when one of the parents was hostile to the idea. Importantly, the President of the Family Court Division added that it was not necessary to show that exceptional circumstances exist before a shared Residence Order may be granted.[26]

The Judge went on to say that an application for Joint Residence must satisfy the Court that it is in the interest of the child in accordance with the requirements of Welfare Checklist that such an order is made.

A further piece of case law which addresses the common misconception that Joint Residence Orders are only awarded when parents agree, was the case which saw a bitterly contested custody battle being finally resolved when the Judge ordered that the parents share residence.[27]

2.5 EMERGENCY PROTECTION ORDER

What is an Emergency Protection Order?

An Emergency Protection Order is an order that lasts for eight days.[28] The order allows for the removal of children from their current accommodation into the care of the applicant and accommodation provided by the applicant. The order can be then extended for a further seven days.[29] As the name suggests, this type of order is only relevant to 'emergency' situations where it is considered that there is significant risk to the children.

It sets out that anyone in a position to produce the child to the applicant must do so and allows for the removal of the child to the applicant's care.[30]

The order temporarily grants the applicant Parental Responsibility for the children if the applicant doesn't already have it.[31]

The order can restrict or place conditions on contact between the children and anyone named in the order, and can direct that an assessment be carried out which can include medical and psychiatric examination of the children.[32]

An amendment made to the Children Act 1989, included in the Family Law Act 1996, allows for the child to remain in their location, but for an adult to be removed if this will ensure that the child is likely to cease to suffer significant harm and can include the power of arrest if the person who has been excluded breaches the order.[33]

Can I apply for an Emergency Protection Order?

While Social Services are most likely to request this type of order, anyone can apply to the Court if they believe that children are likely to suffer significant harm if the order isn't made, and that the child will likely suffer harm if they don't remain with the applicant.[34]

When might an Emergency Protection Order be made?

As mentioned previously, when the children are considered to be at risk of significant harm. Examples of the circumstances where such an order would be applicable can include neglect, domestic violence or sexual abuse.

Are there other circumstances in which this type of order is made?

An Emergency Protection Order can also be used to prevent children being removed from their current location. An example of a situation in which this would apply would be if a parent intended to remove their child from a hospital preventing treatment, and their doing so would cause the child significant harm.[35]

Why does the order only last eight days?

Where a child is considered to be at risk, the Court has to make a fast decision to ensure the child is protected. This often doesn't allow the respondent time to defend against the order, and they may not even be aware that the matter is before the Court. The accused person could find themself ordered from their home and threatened with arrest if they return.

During the eight day period, investigations can be started to confirm the nature of risk to the child, or the harm they have suffered. These can be carried out while the child is in a safe environment.

During those eight days, both the applicant and respondent to the Emergency Protection Order have the opportunity to make other applications to the Court.

If the respondent wasn't notified of, and didn't attend, the hearing where the decision to make the order was made, they can seek to have the order overturned (cancelled) and the child returned to their care. They can make this application to the Court after 72 hours have elapsed from the time the order was made.[36]

Either you, as the applicant, or your ex-partner, as the respondent, could apply for a Residence Order allowing the child to live with you permanently and a Contact Order to regulate the amount and type of contact that they have with their other parent (if they are the respondent).

What may happen if Social Services become involved?

Regardless of whether the Court orders an assessment, Social Services have a duty to commence an investigation into the children's circumstances when the Court makes an Emergency Protection Order.[37]

If Social Services are asked to carry out an assessment by the Court, there is a possibility they could apply to take over responsibility for the Emergency Protection Order if they believe it to be in the best interests of the children concerned. The Court will then treat Social Services as if they had been granted the Court Order.[38]

An Emergency Protection Order cannot be transferred in favour of Social Services if the children are in a refuge, since a refuge is considered to be a place of safety.

What would Social Services consider before applying to take over the Order?

Social Services have a duty to discuss such steps with the original applicant for the Emergency Protection Order. They must base such a decision on the principles set out in the Welfare Checklist, the opinion of the Court, the reasons for the original application, and will take into account the nature of the relationship between the applicant and the children.[39]

As an example, a set of circumstances that could result in Social Services taking over an order could be where a neighbour of the family made the application after having witnessed neglect. In the event that the order was granted as neglect was proved, but the neighbour couldn't provide a suitable level of care, a transfer of the order would be in the children's best interests.

Understandably, if there is concern that the children would suffer significant harm in the care of both the respondent and the applicant, Social Services should take over the order.

Are there circumstances where an Emergency Protection Order is made but the children aren't recovered?

Yes. If the children are living in a refuge, then it may be considered that the children are already in a place of safety.[40] In these circumstances, consider an application for a Residence Order.

2.6 RECOVERY ORDER

What is a Recovery Order?

Recovery Orders provide legal measures to assist in the recovery of children who have been unlawfully taken away from the person who is responsible for them. A Recovery Order may also be made if the children have run away, or are missing.[41]

Can I apply for a Recovery Order?

You can apply for a Recovery Order if an Emergency Protection Order has been granted in your favour.[42]

If no Residence Order is in place and your ex-partner has removed your children from the family home, an application for a Residence Order would be the appropriate order to request.

If you consider your children to be at risk of significant harm in your ex-partner's care, then an Emergency Protection Order should be applied for, following which a Recovery Order can be made. As an alternative to going to Court, you should notify Social Services which can investigate your concerns.

What measures does the order provide to assist in the return of my children?

A Recovery Order directs anyone in possession of the children to produce them when requested to do so by someone authorised by the Court. An authorised person could be anyone who the Court deems suitable, including yourself if you are the applicant.

The order permits the removal of the children by the authorised person and requires anyone who has information about the children's whereabouts to divulge it when asked by the Police or an Officer of the Court.

The order also authorises the Police to use reasonable force to enable them to search for the children and to enter premises where the Court believes the children might be.[43]

What happens if people withhold information about the children's whereabouts and attempt to prevent them from being recovered?

They will be committing an offence and the Court can impose fines as a punishment.[44]

What happens if the Police become involved?

Before returning the child to the applicant, or giving the applicant any information as to the whereabouts of the child, the Police must check their records to see whether either party has committed acts of violence. Having located the child, then without notifying the applicant of the child's whereabouts, they may make enquiries with regard to the child's welfare.

If, when the Police check their records, they find that the applicant has a history of violence, or they have concerns about returning the child to the applicant's care, the Police will not remove the child. They may also advise the respondent to seek legal representation and must notify the Court of their action immediately.

If there is no record of violence and no reason to believe that the applicant is a risk to the children, the Police will return the child to the applicant.

2.7 PROHIBITED STEPS ORDER

What is a Prohibited Steps Order?

Prohibited Steps Orders relate to restricting Parental Responsibility. If a parent has parental responsibility, then he or she has the right independently to take decisions about matters such as schooling, medical treatment, and religion. A Prohibited Steps Order can remove a parent's right to make such decisions about their child's life.[13]

This type of order may also be used to prevent a parent with a Residence Order in their favour from removing their children from the jurisdiction of the Court (England and Wales).

Who can apply for a Prohibited Steps Order?

Any parent, guardian or holder of a Residence Order in relation to the children can apply for a Prohibited Steps Order.[14]

Are there any situations where a Prohibited Steps Order wouldn't be granted?

There is one restriction: the Court cannot make a Prohibited Steps Order where a Residence or Contact Order could address the issues that prompted the application.[45]

As an example, if you were wishing to prevent your ex-partner from having face-to-face contact with your children due to concerns that the children could suffer abuse, you should apply for a Residence Order, and a Contact Order restricting the type of contact to indirect contact.

If you wanted to prevent the other parent from taking the children abroad, a Residence Order in your favour would achieve this.

Naturally, the Court's willingness to grant the order will depend on the circumstances presented to them and what the Court considers to be in the children's best interests.

2.8 SPECIFIC ISSUE ORDER

What is a Specific Issue Order?

As its name suggests, this type of order is used when the Court is asked to resolve an issue relating to the children, other than residence or contact, where parents cannot agree.[13]

Who can apply for a Specific Issue Order?

Any parent, guardian or holder of a Residence Order in relation to the children can apply for a Specific Issue Order.[14]

What issues could this type of order address?

This type of order would be applicable were you and your ex-partner unable to agree which school to send your children to, whether the children should go to a particular place of worship, or if either parent wished to ask the Court's permission to change a child's name.

If you had a Residence Order made in your favour, and you wanted to take the children abroad for more than a month, you would need to get the Court's permission by way of a Specific Issue Order if your ex-partner objected.

Similarly, if you were the non-resident parent, and you wanted to take your children on holiday and your ex-partner objected, you should approach the Court to ask their permission. You would do this by applying for a Specific Issue Order.

2.9 FAMILY ASSISTANCE ORDER

What is a Family Assistance Order?

A Court can make a Family Assistance Order as a means of providing social work support to families experiencing difficulties after separation or divorce.[46] The Court conveys a duty on the Social Worker to befriend, advise and assist anyone named in the order. The order can only be made if Social Services agree or if the children concerned live, or will live, within their area.[47]

Who can be named in the order?

The order can include the parents or guardian of the children, the children themselves, and anyone with whom the children live or who are named in a Contact Order allowing contact with the children.[48]

Can I apply for a Family Assistance Order?

No. This type of order is only made when a Judge considers it to be appropriate, rather than when a parent makes a formal application.

It may be possible during the course of an application for another form of order, such as a Residence or Contact Order, to ask the Court to consider making a Family Assistance Order.

When is a Family Assistance Order made?

Family Assistance Orders can only be made in 'exceptional' circumstances and when all the people named in the order are in agreement with it being made.[49] The purpose of the Order is to preserve the children's relationship with their parents.

How long does a Family Assistance Order remain in force?

For six months, or shorter if a time period is specified in the order.[50]

Does the Social Worker have any other role or powers if a Family Assessment Order is made?

Yes. The Social Worker may refer back to the Court and request a variation to any Residence, Contact, Prohibited Steps or Specific Issue Order that is in force in respect of the children named in the Family Assistance Order.[51]

2.10 ENFORCING CONTACT AND RESIDENCE ORDERS

What can I do if a Court Order is broken?

There are two important factors to consider when a Court Order is broken. These are the powers that are available to the Court to enforce the Order and what the Court is most likely to do.

What should I do if the Order is broken?

Record the dates when the Order was broken, and have your solicitor write a letter to the other parent asking for them to comply with the terms stated in the Order. This not only attempts to resolve the situation without going back to Court, but ensures you have a record of the Order being broken.

Taking a Contact Order as an example, a single breach shouldn't necessitate a return to Court. There may be valid reasons for contact not going ahead, such as the children being ill. It is only if the breaches are persistent that you should then consider a return to Court to ask a Judge to either enforce, or attach a penalty notice to, the Order. A penalty notice (or penal notice) will clearly inform a parent of what will happen if they break the terms of the Order again.

Similarly, if a non-resident parent didn't return a child after normal weekend staying contact due to the child running a high temperature, a Court may well accept that the non-resident parent was acting in the child's best interests.

What can the Court do if there is a breach of a Residence Order?

Residence Orders (including shared Residence Orders) may be enforced by an application to the Court. The Court can instruct any person in breach of the Order to produce the child to the person with the Residence Order, or empower an Officer of the Court or the Police to take charge of, and hand over, the child. A daily fine can be imposed while the breach continues. Committal to prison is also an option, although rarely used.[52]

Prior to any enforcement action being taken, a copy of the Residence Order should be served on the person who is in breach of the terms of the Order.[53]

If the non-resident parent still refuses to return the child, the Court may make a Recovery Order to facilitate the child's return to the resident parent.

What can the Court do if there is a breach of a Contact Order?

If the resident parent fails to make the child available for contact, the Court has the power to impose a fine, empower a Court Official to take charge of taking the child to see the contact parent, or change the Residence Order in favour of the contact parent. The Court also has the power to commit the resident parent to prison.

What is a Court likely to do?

While the Court has the power to commit a parent to prison for breaking a Contact Order, they are highly unlikely to do so. It can be reasonably argued that the removal of the resident parent to prison is not in the best interests of the child and could cause hostilities between the child and the non-resident parent.[54]

Similarly, the Court is unlikely to impose a fine on the resident parent, since it can be reasonably argued that to do so would disadvantage the child.

The Court can attach a penal notice to the Contact Order, setting out clearly what will happen to the Resident Parent if they break the order again.

The Court may consider altering the terms of the Contact Order if the resident parent reasonably argues that the current arrangements are unworkable.

With regard to changing the Residence Order in favour of the non-resident parent, this would only be considered on the grounds that it would be in the child's best interests according to the principles of the Welfare Checklist.

Both the legal profession and Parliament recognise that the current powers available to the Courts to deal with breaches of Contact Orders are too punitive, limiting the Courts' ability to resolve disputes, since the punishments they can impose are likely to have an adverse effect on the child.

Discussions are being held in Parliament to increase the Courts' powers to include a far wider range of penalties including community service and the imposition of curfews. There is also an intention to include non-punitive measures aimed at resolving conflict through a wider use of Family Assistance Orders and having parents attend parenting classes, counselling and guidance sessions.[55]

3

PARENTAL RESPONSIBILITY AND RIGHTS

Several pieces of legislation outline your rights in Parental Responsibility including the Children Act 1989, the Access to Health Records Act 1990, the Education Act 1996, and to a lesser extent, the Human Rights Act.

What is Parental Responsibility?

The legal definition of Parental Responsibility is "All the rights, duties, powers, responsibilities and authority which by law a parent of a child has in relation to a child and his property." [56]

What does that mean in practice?

Parental Responsibility affords the legal right to take decisions about such things as your children's education, medical matters and religion. Having Parental Responsibility also grants you the automatic right to apply for, or to be involved in, Court Orders that affect your children. This can include matters such as adoption, contact issues involving other family members, care applications by Social Services, changes to your child's surname and appointment of a guardian in the event of the death of their other parent.

Does Parental Responsibility affect whether I have to pay maintenance for my child?

No. The two matters of having legal Parental Responsibility, and being a biological parent with a duty to contribute to your child's maintenance, are entirely unrelated.[57]

By having Parental Responsibility, will I be included in matters that affect my children's lives?

Not necessarily. Either parent with Parental Responsibility has the right to independently make decisions that affect their children. There is, however, an obligation on any person exercising a parental responsibility or parental right to have regard to the views of any other person with the same rights and responsibilities.[58]

If I can't agree with my ex-partner on matters such as schooling or education, what happens?

If you consider the matter to be serious, you can approach the Court to make a Specific Issue Order to resolve the matter.

Will professionals such as doctors and teachers respect my right to be included in decisions that affect my children's lives?

They should, but some professionals are ignorant of parents' rights and their own duty to uphold those rights. This can be a particular problem for non-resident parents, or, in the case of parents with joint residence, where the children live for a majority of the time with their other parent.

Information is included in this Chapter to help you to remind professionals of what your rights are.

3.1 HOW TO OBTAIN PARENTAL RESPONSIBILITY

As a biological parent, do I have Parental Responsibility for my child?

A mother automatically has Parental Responsibility for her child. A father may not, depending on whether he was married to the mother at the time of the child's birth or subsequently.

How do I obtain Parental Responsibility for my child?

You obtain parental responsibility in the following ways:[59]

1. By being the child's mother (automatic).
2. By having been married to the child's mother if you are the biological father.
3. If you aren't married but the child was born on or after 1 December 2003 and you jointly registered the birth of your child.[60]
4. By having a Residence Order made in your favour by the Court.
5. If you don't have parental responsibility granted to you by any of these four possibilities as the biological father, you can get Parental Responsibility by signing an official agreement with your child's mother if she will agree to this. A separate agreement is needed for each child.

How do I make a Parental Responsibility Agreement?

The agreement must be written out in the correct format. A copy of the form to use is available from Her Majesty's Court Service. You could also ask your local Family Court for assistance.

The agreement must be signed in front of a Justice of the Peace (Magistrate), Justices' Clerk or a Court official who is authorised by the Judge to administer oaths.

You will need to complete the Parental Responsibility Agreement and present it along with the child's full birth certificate and photographic evidence identifying both parents (ideally a photo driving licence or passport) to a Family Proceedings Court, County Court, or the Principal Registry of the Family Division where it can be signed and witnessed.

Two copies must then be made, and sent along with the original to the Principal Registry of the Family Division.

As a mother, can I make this Agreement with the child's stepfather?

No. Only biological parents can enter into a Parental Responsibility Agreement.

What do I do if my child's mother won't sign an Agreement?

If the mother refuses to sign a Parental Responsibility Agreement, you can apply to the Court asking them to grant you parental responsibility by making a Parental Responsibility Order in your favour. The form to use is the C1, available from Her Majesty's Court Service.

If you can afford it, hire a solicitor to assist you in completing the paperwork, organising a Court hearing and representing you in Court. Consider whether you could apply for legal aid.

The Court will charge a fee regardless of whether you're represented by a solicitor or not.

As a father, are there any organisations that can help me if I can't afford a solicitor and don't qualify for Legal Aid?

Yes. Families Need Fathers provides information and advice on matters such as obtaining parental responsibility. Although the name suggests that the organisation only assists fathers, it provides a similar service for mothers.

What will the Court consider when deciding whether to grant my application?

The following points are likely to be considered by the Court when assessing your application for a Parental Responsibility Order:

- whether your name appears on the birth certificate.
- how active you have been in maintaining contact with your children and meeting your commitments to them.
- your previous involvement in your children's education.
- what financial support you provide for your children.
- the reasons for your application.
- the strength of the relationship between you and your children and the degree of commitment you've previously shown to your children.

The Court will also consider the principles set down in the Welfare Checklist.

Is the Court likely to grant an application for Parental Responsibility?

Yes. Less than 2% of applications made to the Courts in 2004 and 2005 were refused.[61]

3.2 YOUR RIGHT TO MEDICAL INFORMATION

Do I have a right to ask to see my children's medical records?

Yes. Health professionals must provide information when an application is made by an individual with parental responsibility where the child is under the age of sixteen.[62]

If you have Parental Responsibility for your children, a medical practitioner is legally obliged to see you when you request this, and to discuss matters relating to your children's health.

What types of health professionals are covered by the Access to Health Records Act?

The term "health professional" includes the following registered practitioners:[63]

- a General Practitioner
- a Dentist
- an Optician
- a Pharmaceutical Chemist
- a Nurse, Midwife or Health Visitor
- a Chiropodist, Dietician, Occupational Therapist, Orthoptist or Physiotherapist
- a Clinical Psychologist, Child Psychotherapist or Speech Therapist

- an Art or Music Therapist employed by a health service body

Are there circumstances where the health professional can refuse to share information with me?

Yes. Unless the health professional considers the child to be too young to understand the nature of your application and that it is in their best interest that information is shared with you, the health professional can only pass on information if they have the child's consent.[64]

An example of circumstances where a doctor may feel it inappropriate to share your child's records would be where a fifteen-year-old girl had approached the doctor for birth control advice, and the child wanted the matter to be treated in confidence.

The health professional may withhold information if they consider that disclosing it would cause serious harm to the physical or mental health of their patient or any other individual.[65]

A further scenario where information could be withheld is where your child's record contains information about another individual, and to share this record with you would break that other person's right to confidentiality unless you had their consent.[66]

Where one parent is involved in decisions about medical treatment, is the other parent entitled to be involved?

Yes. Your views should be taken into account so long as they are deemed to be in the child's best interests.

Will my consent be required if my child needs medical treatment?

Consent to treatment is only normally required from one person with parental responsibility.

At what age is my child's opinion considered relevant to matters involving the disclosure of information and consent to medical treatment?

In England and Wales, no legislation specifically sets out the rights of children under sixteen to give their consent to medical treatment, so there remains some uncertainty about this in common law.

In the landmark Victoria Gillick case, the Judges held that "parental rights were recognised by the law so long as they were needed for the protection of the child and such rights yielded to the child's right to make his own decisions when he reached a sufficient understanding and intelligence to be capable of making up his own mind".[67] This has become known in law as the Gillick Principle.

Circumstances where a doctor would consider this principle would be where a girl under the age of sixteen asked the doctor for contraceptive advice.

What do I do if I don't know who my children's doctor is?

If you are unable to find out which doctor your children are registered with, you can contact the children's Local Area Health Authority (or Primary Care Trust).

The Local Area Health Authority must provide written details stating where the children are registered to anyone with parental responsibility for the children.

How should I contact the Local Area Health Authority?

Make the request in writing. Include proof of your parental responsibility in relation to the children by providing the Authority with either a copy of your Marriage Certificate, the children's Birth Certificates or a copy of any Parental Responsibility Orders made in your favour.

How should I approach a health professional for information about my children?

It may be more expedient to write to the medical professional to request information. Include a copy of your Marriage Certificate or Parental Responsibility Order. In the event your request is refused, you will have proof that a request was made.

What happens if the medical practitioner refuses my request?

They may have good reason to decide not to disclose information to you. Should your request be refused, ask the professional concerned for information about how you can make a complaint.

You could consider making a complaint to either to the head of the medical practice (such as the Practice Manager), the Local Area Health Authority or to the professional organisation to which the health professional belongs (such as the General Medical Council in the case of General Practitioners).

3.3 YOUR RIGHT TO INVOLVEMENT IN YOUR CHILD'S SCHOOLING

As a parent, do I have a right to be involved in my children's schooling?

Yes. Under education legislation any parent (regardless of whether they hold Parental Responsibility for the children), has the following rights to involvement in their children's schooling:[68]

1. To participate in decisions about their child's education (e.g. deciding which subjects the child should study).
2. To be treated equally to any other parent by the school and Local Education Authority (LEA) staff.
3. To receive information from the school (e.g. copies of the governors' annual report, pupil reports and attendance records).
4. To participate in certain school activities (e.g. vote in elections for parent governors, attend sports days and school performances).
5. To be asked for their consent for their children to take part in extra-curricular activities.
6. To be advised about meetings involving the child (e.g. where a governors' meeting is being held to discuss the possibility of a child's exclusion from school for bad behaviour).
7. To be included on an equal basis with the other parent in their children's school records.

What are the school's responsibilities to parents?

1. To note the details of Court Orders on the pupil's record.

2. Not to allow the name of the child to be changed without the consent of every other person with parental responsibility for the child.

3. To ask the resident parent for the address details of the non-resident parent.

4. To make the resident parent aware that the other parent is entitled to be involved in the child's education.

5. To keep address records for all parents / guardians in the admission register and any written or computerised pupil records, and passing this information on to any new school that a child may attend.

6. To provide information to a parent directly if that parent requests such information.

7. To seek parental consent in relation to extra-curricular activities.

8. To uphold the principle that parental consent has not been given in relation to the child undertaking activities if one parent gives consent and the other withholds it.

9. To inform the resident parent as soon as possible when a child has had an accident and the non-resident parent, if they have asked to be kept informed, of events involving the child.

10. To consider the welfare of the child to be paramount and try to resolve problems without becoming involved in conflict.

11. To involve parents in issues relating to their child's education.

12. To keep parents informed about school matters.

What can I do if the school refuses to grant me these rights?

Refer the Headmaster or Headmistress to the Guidance for Head Teachers published by the Department for Education and Skills.[69]

If you still have problems, the chain of complaint for maintained schools (state schools) about issues such as admissions policy, behaviour, exclusions and non-receipt of information is: Headteacher, Chair of the governing body, LEA, then the Department for Education and Skills.

Advice is available from the National Education Law Advice Line which provides legal advice and representation to children and/or parents with concerns relating to schools or Local Education Authorities.

Will I need to prove I am the child's parent?

Possibly, but under Education Act legislation you only need to prove you are the biological parent. A copy of a birth certificate naming you as the parent or a letter from the Child Support Agency showing you make maintenance payments in respect of your child should be sufficient to prove parentage.

3.4 YOUR RIGHT TO INVOLVEMENT IN A CHILD'S EARLY EDUCATION

Do I have a right to receive information about my children in relation to their Early Years Education?

Anyone providing Early Years Education, be it in a child minder, crèche, nursery, playgroup or day care setting, must be registered with the Office for Standards in Education (Ofsted). Part of the criteria for registration is that the organisation must adhere to a set of national standards.[70]

Different standards are published for child minding, full day care, sessional care, out-of-school care and crèches. Within each guidance document, National Standard 12 sets out the Child Minder's responsibility to work in partnership with parents to meet the children's needs and to share information.[71] The supporting criteria vary for each type of childcare provider, and you should contact Ofsted to ask for a copy of the relevant set of standards.

The Glossary section within each National Standard document defines a parent as "anyone who holds Parental Responsibility for a child".

What do I do if the standards are not followed?

The childcare provider has a duty to investigate your complaint. You have several routes of complaint that you can pursue if the playgroup won't address your concerns.

You could raise a complaint with Ofsted Early Years that the childcare provider is in breach of the National Standards.

If Ofsted won't pursue your complaint, or suggest it's a contractual matter between parents and the playgroup, contact your Member of Parliament and have them challenge Ofsted's interpretation of the National Standards (which make no distinction between either parent other than a need to have Parental Responsibility for the children).

Contact the LEA to find out if the childcare provider is LEA maintained or private. If they are LEA maintained, you can ask the LEA to provide you with a copy of your child's educational record.[72]

3.5 OTHER MATTERS - RELIGION, CORPORAL PUNISHMENT

Do I have the right to choose my children's religion?

Yes, although where two parents disagree over the choice of religious upbringing for their children, the considerations regarding the children's welfare will prevail should the Court become involved in resolving the conflict.

A religion cannot be imposed on a child if the Court considered that the child would suffer harm as a result of following the religion's tenets. As an example, if a religion stated that a follower shouldn't receive modern medical treatment, the Court may decide the imposition of that belief could cause the child harm.

Can my children choose their own religion?

The Human Rights Act 1998 protects the children's right to make their own decisions as it protects the individual's right to the freedom of thought, conscience and religion.[73]

A child who is sufficiently mature to take the decision as to which religion they wish to follow may do so (according to the Gillick principle).

Is my consent required if my children wish to marry?

Where the child is aged between 16 and 18 they can only marry if all parties with parental responsibility agree unless the Court is approached to consider the matter as a Specific Issue.

Can anyone change my children's name?

No, unless they have the agreement of all the parties with parental responsibility for the child or the Court give their permission by way of a Specific Issue Order.[74]

Can my child leave home without my consent?

Children under the age of sixteen cannot leave home without parental consent.

Is it legal to use corporal punishment to discipline your child?

Individuals with parental responsibility have the legal right to use "reasonable" physical punishment. It is illegal to punish a child to the extent that the child is a victim of battery, suffers grievous bodily harm, actual bodily harm or experiences punishment that could be considered to be cruelty.[75] Essentially, if you have Parental Responsibility you can smack your child as a form of punishment, but if the smack leaves a mark you may be found guilty of causing actual bodily harm.

Can I take my child abroad?

Where a Residence Order is in force, non-resident parents cannot take their children abroad without the written consent of all other parties who have parental responsibility unless they have the Court's permission to do so. A resident parent automatically has the right to take their children abroad for a period of up to one month.[76]

3.6 TIPS FOR MAKING COMPLAINTS

Regardless of your legal rights, even when you've informed someone of those rights, you may find that a professional such as a teacher, doctor, or nursery manager still won't give you information.

In the event that a professional won't share information with you about your children, you have the choice of either backing down or asking a Court to make a Specific Issue Order to resolve the issue. Use your discretion as to which battles are worth fighting.

The various legal acts and guidelines included in this section should assist you in clarifying to the Court why you feel entitled to this information.

When attempting to have your rights granted to you, I would recommend you go through the following stages:

1. Make an initial phone call, or visit. Ask for the information, remaining calm. Make a note of who you spoke to, your discussion and the time and date of the phone call

2. If the information is refused, ask for the name of the person in charge (if you're not currently speaking to them) and their address. This could be the Head of Surgery, the Headmaster, or Playgroup Manager

3. Write a simple letter, referring back to the conversation and once again asking for the information. Explain why you're entitled to it, including a reference to the relevant legislation in this chapter. Include details of the previous verbal conversation.

4. If they continue to refuse, ask them how you can make an official

complaint. Most agencies have an official complaints procedure

5. Follow the procedure, but if you still don't have any luck you could consider:

> a) a complaint to the Information Commissioner. Under the Data Protection Act 1998 you may be entitled to information held about your child.[77] You could contact the Information Commissioner to check on this, and to make a complaint.

> b) contact your Member of Parliament. If you feel your parental rights have been curtailed, and a government department is being either lethargic or obstructive, it can be quite surprising how quickly a file is "re-opened" when the people concerned hear that an MP is involved.

6. You could instruct your solicitor to send a letter to the organisation setting out your rights and asking that they be recognised.

7. Finally, when you've exhausted other avenues, you have the option of taking the matter to Court to ask the Court to address the situation.

4

EXPERT WITNESSES AND BEING ASSESSED

In this chapter we look at three different expert witnesses who may be called to appear before the Court. These chapters look specifically at the role of the Social Worker, CAFCASS Officer and Forensic Psychologist in private family law cases.

An expert may be asked by the Court to provide an impartial opinion on any relevant matter for which they are qualified to give evidence. This could be a doctor commenting on physical injuries to a child, a Forensic Psychologist on a parent's mental health, or a Social Worker or CAFCASS officer on the family dynamics and circumstances.

If you believe that an expert witness is required to support your case, you need to ask the permission of the Court. A child who is the subject of proceedings under the Children Act 1989 may not be medically or psychiatrically examined, or otherwise assessed for the purposes of preparing expert evidence, without the permission of the Court.

If a Court were to refuse to allow you to call on expert testimony, this could be a breach of your right to a fair trial and give you grounds for an appeal.

Where an expert witness is required, the Court will encourage both the Applicant and Respondent to jointly instruct an expert (reach agreement on which expert is to be used and to set out on what the expert should give their opinion or assessment).

4.1 SOCIAL SERVICES

Why would Social Services become involved in my case?

The Court may ask for Social Services to provide information to assist the Judge in considering matters relating to the welfare of your children.

If Social Services have previously been involved with your family, it is possible that the Court will ask them to provide a report on the circumstances that led to their involvement, and the current situation (if they are still involved).[78]

Does a Social Services report for the Court have a special name?

Yes, the report would be referred to as a Section 7 Report.[79]

Do Social Services have to provide a report if the Court requests them to do so?

Yes.[80]

What can I do if there is information in the report that is incorrect, or if the Social Worker expresses an opinion that I disagree with?

If you believe there is information included in the Section 7 Report that is inaccurate or false, then your solicitor or barrister can challenge the Social Worker's opinions. The Judge can grant leave for the Social Worker to be called for cross-examination.

Could I complain to the Local Government Ombudsman if Social Services make mistakes relating to the Section 7 Report?

No. Normally, you can complain to the Local Government Ombudsman in the event that Social Services make a mistake, but the Ombudsman will not investigate any matter that is before a Court in private law proceedings. The place to challenge what Social Services have said is before the Court.

Are there any other reasons the Court may direct Social Services to become involved with my family during the course of a Family Law case?

Yes. When an Emergency Protection Order is made, Social Services will be informed, as the children named in the Order will be considered to be at risk of significant harm.[81] If CAFCASS become involved at the request of the Court, and Social Services have been involved with the family in the past, it is likely that Social Services will be contacted by them.

Are there any organisations that provide information and advice to families who are dealing with Social Services?

Yes. The Family Rights Group are a registered charity and provide advice and support for families whose children are involved with Social Services.

Is there anything else to be aware of?

Yes, it is worthwhile obtaining a copy of the guidelines that the Social Worker should adhere to. The document which sets out the standards which Social Services should follow both in terms of how they treat your family, and how they conduct investigations is called The Framework for the Assessment of Children in Need and their Families.[82]

4.2 CAFCASS

What does CAFCASS stand for?

The Children and Family Court Advisory and Support Service (CAFCASS).

What is CAFCASS?

CAFCASS is an organisation which looks after the welfare of children involved in Family Law proceedings. A CAFCASS Officer (also called Family Reporter) is trained in social work but independent from Social Services. They carry out a number of different duties including mediation, investigation into family circumstances and also make recommendations to the Court.

Examples of recommendations which they may make include:

- which parent the children should live with
- arrangements for contact with the non-resident parent
- the type(s) of Order which the CAFCASS Officer considers relevant to the family circumstance.

Why would CAFCASS become involved in my Court case?

In private Family Law proceedings, CAFCASS would become involved for two main reasons:

1. To provide a mediation service to the separating parents in

an attempt to find agreement without the need for the Court's involvement

2. When the Judge wants an independent and objective assessment of the family's situation.

How important is the CAFCASS Officer's recommendation to the Court?

While the Judge ultimately decides what will happen to the children, the CAFCASS Officer's recommendation will carry a great deal of weight with the Court, especially since the Judge will consider their opinion to be impartial and focussed on the children's needs. For this reason it is important to familiarise yourself with their role and the standards they are supposed to adhere to.

What are the standards which CAFCASS should adhere to?

CAFCASS works to standards set out in a document called the *Service Principles and Standards.*[83]

When CAFCASS have concluded an investigation, they will write a report for the Judge. This report could include details of the family's circumstances, the wishes of the parents and children and the CAFCASS Officer's opinion as to the outcome which would be in the children's best interests.

In relation to the report, it is important to be aware of the standards that CAFCASS should adhere to. The CAFCASS Officer should:

- set out all relevant information which the CAFCASS Officer has acquired through his or her enquiries, making clear from which source the information has been obtained and distinguishing between matters of fact and opinion.

- make clear recommendations (or explain why recommendations cannot be made) which draw on relevant aspects of the Welfare Checklist.

- explain the basis upon which those recommendations have been made, including reasons both for and against those recommendations.

- consider all orders available to the Court when making a recommendation.

Will the CAFCASS Officer treat what I say in confidence?

If CAFCASS are asked to mediate between you and your ex-partner, then what you say during discussions with them is private.

In the event that agreement isn't reached (and the matter returns to Court for the case to continue), CAFCASS may be asked to continue their involvement by carrying out an investigation for the Court. In these circumstances a different Officer should be appointed from the one who facilitated mediation.

Will I see a copy of the report before the Court hearing?

The CAFCASS Officer has a duty to provide the parents and children with as much information as possible regarding the proposed report content and recommendations.

At the hearing where the Judge instructs CAFCASS to carry out an investigation, the Judge will set a timetable which should detail when the report should be filed with the Court and sent to each parent's solicitor. Court rules state this should be at least five days before the hearing where the recommendations of the report will be considered.[84]

If you have not received the report by the date set out in the timetable, contact the Children and Family Reporter as a matter of urgency and discuss the delay with your solicitor. Ensure you have sufficient time to consider what the CAFCASS Officer has said in their report.

What happens if I disagree with the findings and recommendations of the report?

If you disagree with the recommendations within the report or find it contains factual inaccuracies, raise your concerns with your solicitor. You could write to the CAFCASS Officer pointing out your concerns or have your solicitor ask the Court's permission to make a responding statement. Unless the Judge excuses the CAFCASS Officer from attending the hearing, the CAFCASS Officer should be present to discuss the contents of their report.[85] Your solicitor or barrister should also have the opportunity during the course of the proceedings to cross-examine them.[86]

How long does a CAFCASS investigation take?

The investigation is normally concluded within ten weeks.[87]

4.3 FORENSIC PSYCHOLOGISTS

What is a Forensic Psychologist?

Forensic Psychologists specialise in the area where law and psychology meet. They carry out psychological evaluations, write reports setting out their findings, and attend Court to give expert testimony.

Can a psychiatrist or psychologist carry out the assessment if they don't have forensic training?

Yes, but while the quality of any assessment may be to a similar standard, a Forensic Psychologist also has experience in attending Court and writing reports for the Court to consider. A report that is ambiguous or confusing may be misinterpreted or found to be inconclusive, requiring further assessments to be carried out. This may delay or prevent the Court from having sufficient information to make a decision.

Can I ask the Court to order that my ex-partner be psychologically assessed?

Yes, but the Court will only consider such a request if there are good reasons.

When would a Forensic Psychologist carry out an investigation?

The Court may consider requesting a psychological evaluation when allegations of mental illness or personality disorder need to be investigated.

The primary causes for the Court to order the evaluation would be where it is alleged that behaviour attributed to mental health poses a risk to the other parent or the children (or both) or may otherwise impact on the children's welfare.

What should the evaluation include?

Ensure your solicitor requests that the following questions are covered by the psychological evaluation and subsequent report:

- Does the person being assessed suffer from a mental illness or mental disorder?

- To what extent is it possible that any condition found could affect parenting ability?

- What risks does the condition carry for the children, both in terms of physical risk and the potential for emotional and psychological harm?

- Is there a potential impact on the child's development and the parent's ability to provide consistent care?

- Is treatment/medication an option, and what treatments would the psychologist recommend?

- Is the condition manageable?

- To what extent does the psychologist believe treatment could be effective and what timescales would the psychologist deem "normal" for treatment of any condition identified?

- What services are available?

Common sense also dictates that the longer and more detailed the assessment, the more accurate it is likely to be. An assessment carried out over several sessions may identify behaviour that isn't apparent in a single interview.

What should I tell the Court or the psychologist if I ask for an assessment?

If you have noticed a pattern to your partner's behaviour, ensure that the assessor is made aware of this. You may have the opportunity to do this if you are included in the assessment. If you aren't, the psychologist should become aware of your observations and experiences if you included this information in your original statement.

If your ex-partner has a diagnosed condition, has previously received treatment or has a history of mental health problems, this should also be included in your first statement to the Court.

What will the psychologist do?

The psychological assessment will include one or more face-to-face assessments. It may include psychological tests, which are designed to identify mental illness or personality disorders depending on the type of test carried out.

What is a psychological test?

Psychological tests (known as 'personality inventories') are questionnaires designed to identify whether the person being assessed has thoughts and behaviours that indicate they have a personality disorder or clinical illness.

The statements included in the questionnaires cover a wide range of topics, including attitudes on religion, sexual practices, perceptions of health, political ideas, information on family, education and occupation. The questionnaire identifies symptoms that are exhibited by people suffering from certain forms of mental disorder.

These tools are commonly used by psychologists or psychiatrists to help carry out psychological evaluations.

If I ask for a psychological assessment how much will it cost?

Psychological assessments are expensive and you can expect to pay several thousand pounds. If you are eligible for legal aid, this may cover the cost.

How do I find a Forensic Psychologist?

There are a number of different ways to find a Forensic Psychologist. The Court may recommend one or you could ask your solicitor or barrister if they can recommend one they have worked with in the past (and respect). You can also look for one on the British Psychological Society website where you can see details of their qualifications and areas of expertise.

As with any professional, some are more suitable than others and have a better reputation. Your solicitor's or barrister's recommendation is important, since they will have seen the quality of reports previously provided, how the psychologist stands up to cross-examination, whether their findings tend to be ambiguous and open to challenge or whether their reports are precise and well founded.

4.4 TIPS FOR ASSESSMENT INTERVIEWS

When being assessed, regardless of the agency carrying out the evaluation, it is worth considering what you want the assessment to achieve. Your objective should be to provide the assessor with information that assists the Court in making an informed and fair judgment.

It is normal to feel nervous about being evaluated and to be stressed about the Court case, as well as any allegations made, and to be confused about the reasons behind the allegations if they're untrue.

Below are some things to consider before your evaluation.

Do   speak calmly and clearly.

Do   show willingness to partake in the evaluation.

Do   agree to sign any releases or waivers to allow the evaluator any information they need such as a copy of your medical records.

Do   tell the truth.

Do   tell the evaluator of any concerns you have with regard to your child, but also make clear that you want your ex-partner to be fully involved in your child's life and that you understand how important they are in your child's life.

Do   state that you want only what is right for your child.

Do   ensure you cover all the points in the evaluation that you feel are necessary. For your own benefit, write these down, prior to the evaluation, and read it before the meeting.

Don't criticise your ex-partner as a person. If there are
things they do which concern you, explain those actions
and behaviours.

Don't say you wish to stop your ex-partner from seeing
your child. This will be harmful to your child. Risks can
be addressed in other ways, and the evaluator will wish
to make their own recommendations.

Don't make false allegations.

Don't exaggerate.

Don't lose your cool, become angry, or appear unreasonably
emotional.

Don't argue or be sarcastic with the evaluator.

Don't tell the evaluator what to do, or try to lead the sessions.

Understand that where allegations are made, they need to be investigated. This may include psychologists, Social Services, or CAFCASS wishing to talk to your doctor, your children's school, a health visitor, child minder, or any other professional involved with either yourself or your children.

Are there any tips specifically relating to psychological assessments?

If you are taking part in a psychological assessment and are asked to complete a personality inventory:

- read the instructions and questions carefully

- ensure you're filling in the correct columns

- be honest in your answers.

These tests are cleverly constructed and have measures to help the psychologist identify if the person taking the test is trying to cheat or lie.

5

CRISIS SITUATIONS

Some parents who separate find themselves either facing crisis situations or fear their occurrence.

A crisis situation can include:

1. Coming home to find that your house is empty and your ex-partner has left with the children.
2. Your ex-partner taking the children to another country.
3. Being a victim of domestic violence.
4. Fearing your children are suffering sexual abuse.
5. Concerns for your children's welfare due to a parent's mental health.
6. Finding yourself facing false allegations.
7. Your partner suffering from mental illness.
8. Allegations against you being upheld by expert witnesses.
9. The stress of separation and Court proceedings affecting your health.
10. Your children suffering from your separation.

It is normal to feel helpless and powerless in these situations, but you are not.

5.1 DOMESTIC CHILD ABDUCTION

What is domestic abduction?

For the purpose of this section, domestic abduction is where one parent leaves the family home without warning and takes the children with them.

What do I do if I come home to find the house empty?

It is a terrifying situation to come home and find the house is empty. Desertion is thankfully rare, but devastating when your partner has left with your children without warning. Firstly, don't panic.

Most importantly, consider the reasons why you believe your partner has left. Before taking any action you should review the circumstances that led up to their leaving and whether you also believe the relationship to be over:

- It may be that your partner simply needed to get away due to unhappiness about some aspect of their life and they were struggling to cope.

- If you have been guilty of domestic violence, they may have been advised to remove themselves and your children from an abusive situation.

- Your relationship may have been in trouble for some time and they decided that the relationship was over but felt unable to tell you.

When someone leaves without warning, it is usually because they feel the need to take control of their lives.

I still love my ex-partner, what can I do?

Again this depends entirely on the circumstances, and whether you believe that your partner is able to provide a suitable level of care for your children.

If you have no concerns over your partner's mental health, and if there are no 'risk' issues to consider such as alcoholism, drug addiction or abusive behaviour, you have several options:

1. Wait for your partner to make contact.
2. Ask friends or family to intercede on your behalf (if they know where your partner is).
3. Contact a solicitor.

In any relationship experiencing difficulties, communication is the best way to resolve the underlying problems. If you do manage to speak to your partner, or if family and friends will pass on a message on your behalf, show a willingness to listen to the reasons that led to your partner leaving home.

A willingness not only to consider your partner's feelings but also look at and consider changing your own behaviour may help to save your relationship. Couple counselling will help with this, especially when communication has broken down. Importantly, your partner also needs to consider your feelings for the relationship to work, and couple counselling shouldn't be a one-sided process. Contact details for organisations that can help you are in the back of the book.

What can I do if I think there are risks to my children?

If you think your children are at risk, you may find yourself facing mixed emotions. To involve Social Services may jeopardise your relationship with your partner and it may drive a permanent wedge between you (no one likes being told that people don't think they are a safe parent). You have several options and your choice has to be based on your current situation, and the reasons for your concern. If you're not sure what to do, then take advice.

The options are:

1. Phone the National Society for the Prevention of Cruelty to Children. The NSPCC staff are trained Social Workers and will refer you to Social Services if they share your concern. You could also speak to someone at Parentline Plus.
2. Contact your local Social Services Child Protection Unit.
3. Contact the Police.
4. Seek legal representation and go to Court for an Emergency Protection and Recovery Order.

Remember the people with the ultimate responsibility for ensuring children's welfare are the parents. However you're advised, make the decision your decision and try to remain objective. It may help you to sit down with a family member or close friend to discuss what you should do and for emotional support.

What can I do to help trace my children?

If Social Services, the Courts or the Police share your concerns, then provide as much information as you can to help trace them. Filling your time can help you to cope emotionally, especially when you're doing something practical. Put together a pack of the following:

- Your partner's mobile phone number, as well as those of your children if they have them. The Police can very accurately trace the signal from a mobile phone.

- A list of contact details for friends and family including telephone numbers and addresses.

- If your ex-partner works, their employer's address and contact details.

- Recent photographs of your ex-partner and children.

- Bank details for your ex-partner. The use of credit cards can be traced to specific stores and outlets to help locate someone.

- If your ex-partner drives and has taken the car then write down the make, model, colour, and registration number of the vehicle.

- Passport numbers. If you're worried your children may have been taken abroad, refer to the section on International Child Abduction.

Bear in mind that if your ex-partner claims Social Security they will need to give their current address to the Benefits Office. It is very difficult to "disappear" for long.

What are your concerns?

You are more likely to be taken seriously if you can substantiate your concerns (otherwise there may be an inclination to think this is merely a domestic dispute). That doesn't mean that your concerns won't be investigated, but to have your children brought home, you need to be able to show there are sufficient grounds for concern to warrant this. The following risks should be taken very seriously:

1. Drug Addiction. If your partner has an addiction, make the agencies aware of this. If your General Practitioner can confirm this, provide their contact details as well.

2. Alcohol Addiction: as above.

3. Mental Illness. Having a mental illness doesn't mean your ex-partner is incapable of looking after the children, but certain forms of illness may carry risk depending on the severity of the condition. If your partner has a diagnosed mental illness, or has been seeing a therapist, provide details to the agencies while understanding that their illness may have no bearing on their current actions.

4. Mental Disorder: similar to the above.

5. Domestic Violence. If your partner has ever been violent, tell the agencies at this point.

6. Criminal Convictions. Having a criminal record doesn't mean your partner is an unsafe parent, but it may raise additional concern.

7. Corroboration. Is there anyone else who has shared your concern about your partner's behaviour such as friends and family, the school, a child minder, health visitor, GP, counsellor or the playgroup?

Patient confidentiality can be overridden in cases where there is concern of risk to children.

If my children are at risk, should I speak to a solicitor?

If you don't have Parental Responsibility, it is important to speak to a solicitor as soon as possible to make an application to the Court for this to be granted. Once Social Services become involved, it can become a public law matter (not private law), and being a biological parent doesn't mean that your children will automatically come back to live with you if your partner doesn't return to your house.

What will Social Services do?

Social Services' priority won't be to reunite you with your child, but to ensure that your child is safe. If your ex-partner has taken your child to stay with relatives, friends, or is in a refuge, then they may not even inform you of the location of your child. That said, informing Social Services of your concerns may get you some support and immediate action.

Social Services have a duty to take action if they (not you) consider your child to be at risk, or likely to be at risk, of significant harm.[88]

How long will it take Social Services to carry out an assessment?

You'll need to justify your concerns and push for the initial assessment to be undertaken quickly. The guidelines for the speed of response are as follows:

Social Services will decide what form of response is appropriate from them within 24 hours of being contacted. If they do decide to investigate, a brief assessment of your children's circumstances (called an initial assessment) will be carried out within seven days (or earlier depending on the situation).

If a more in-depth assessment is required (called a core assessment) this will usually be concluded within 35 days depending on the need to involve other agencies (such as Mental Health Services).

By choosing to report the matter to Social Services, the speed of response and nature of investigation, together with any decision, is taken out of your hands and the child may not be returned to you. Social Services may decide to go to Court to apply for a number of different orders.

What can the Police do?

If you contact the Police, be clear about what you want them to do. Are you contacting them just to check that your child is safe, or do you firmly believe your child needs to be taken into Police protection?

The Police have specialist officers called Child Protection Officers. The Police have the power to remove a child from their home, or elsewhere if there are concerns about the child's welfare.[89]

The Police can keep a child under Police protection for up to 72 hours.[90] They must inform Social Services as soon as is practically possible and Social Services are responsible for organising accommodation for the child. The Police do not have to inform you of where your child is, however they do have to provide you with the name of the Social Worker handling the case. They also have a duty to tell parents that their child is under Police protection.

You may be able to agree with Social Services that you are best placed to care for your child during this period of time. Alternatively, Social Services may decide to go to Court to apply for an Emergency Protection Order, or to request that the Court make a Supervision or Care Order.

A Care Order allows Social Services to take the children named in the order into care for as long as the order remains in force.[91] A Supervision Order places the child under the supervision of Social Services and the Social Worker will assist, advise and befriend them.[92]

Guidelines for the Police were changed following Lord Laming's inquiry into the death of Victoria Climbié.[93] One important recommendation was that the children should be seen and their circumstances assessed prior to being taken into Police protection.[94]

Can I handle the matter myself?

You can also choose to handle the matter yourself by making a private application to the Court for an Emergency Protection Order and Recovery Order depending on the seriousness of your concern. The benefits of this are:

- If the order is granted in your favour, and you have legal parental responsibility, the child should be returned to your care (unless you have a history of violence or there are serious concerns about your ability to provide adequate care).

- If you don't have parental responsibility you can apply for this at the same time.

- When an Emergency Protection Order is granted, Social Services have a responsibility to carry out an investigation.

- The Emergency Protection Order can include powers to compel anyone else who may know the whereabouts of the children to divulge this information. It also gives the police the power to enter and search premises using reasonable force.

- When a Recovery Order is made, the Police are responsible for returning your children, and will carry out an investigation.

- If the children are missing, and concern exists about their safety, the police will assist in locating them.

What should I ask the solicitor?

When you approach a solicitor to help you, make sure they specialise in family law. Questions to ask should include:

- How quickly can you appear before the Court?

- What will it cost?

- What will happen afterwards? You may then need to apply for a Residence Order, or find yourself as the Respondent if your partner is the one who applies to the Courts for residence of the children.

- What are your chances of having the Emergency Protection and Recovery Orders made in your favour?

- Are you eligible for legal aid?

5.2 INTERNATIONAL CHILD ABDUCTION

What can I do if I'm afraid my ex-partner has taken my child abroad or plans to in the future?

If you are worried that your partner may take your child abroad against your wishes, there are a number of steps you can take to help prevent this. The best place for information and support is from an organisation called Reunite, a UK charity also recommended by the Foreign Office.

Any adult with parental responsibility can order a passport for their child without the permission of the other parent, unless:

1. The other parent has a Residence Order in their favour (under Section 8 of the Children Act 1989).
2. The child is made a Ward of Court, in which case the Court's permission must be sought before a passport can be issued.
3. If the Father doesn't have parental responsibility, then the Mother's permission must be sought before the passport can be issued.
4. A Prohibited Steps Order has been made under the Children Act 1989 preventing this.
5. A Court Order is in force which states that removal of the child from the jurisdiction of the Court is against the Court's wishes.
6. A Court Order is in force stating that your permission is needed before a passport can be issued.

The Passport Office can further advise you on preventing the issue of passports to children.

What do I do if I don't have my children's passports?

If you're not in possession of your child's passport, and you believe your ex-partner will try to remove your child to another country, then seek legal advice.

You could apply to the Court for an Order to prevent a passport being issued in your child's name or a Prohibited Steps Order stating that the other parent cannot take the children abroad or ordering the return of the passports to you.

What do I do if my children have already been taken abroad?

If your child has been taken abroad, contact Reunite. If the children have been taken to a country that is a signatory to the 1980 Hague Convention on the Civil Aspects of International Child Abduction, inform the Department for Constitutional Affairs, Child Abduction Unit.

What is the 1980 Hague Convention on the Civil Aspects of International Child Abduction?

This is an international agreement which seeks to return abducted children to the country where they normally live, so issues of residence and contact can be decided by the Courts of that country.

Which countries are party to the Hague Convention on the Civil Aspects of International Child Abduction?

The countries listed below are signatories to this convention.

Argentina	Germany	Panama
Australia	Greece	Peru
Austria	Honduras	Poland
Bahamas	Hong Kong	Portugal
Belarus	Hungary	Romania
Belgium	Iceland	Serbia and Montenegro
Belize	Ireland	Slovakia
Bosnia and Herzegovina	Israel	Slovenia
Burkina Faso	Italy	South Africa
Canada (most states)	Latvia	Spain
Chile	Liechtenstein	St Kitts & Nevis
Columbia	Lithuania	Sweden
Croatia	Luxembourg	Switzerland
Cyprus (Southern)	Macao	Turkey
Czech Republic	Macedonia	Turkmenistan
Denmark	Malta	Uruguay
Ecuador	Mauritius	United States of America
Estonia	Mexico	Uzbekistan
Fiji	Monaco	Venezuela
Finland	Netherlands	Zimbabwe
France	New Zealand	
Georgia	Norway	

What can the Department for Constitutional Affairs Child Abduction Unit do?

If your child is habitually resident in the UK, and you are a citizen of England or Wales, the Child Abduction Unit may be able to make an application on your behalf under the Hague Convention to the Foreign Central Authority (the relevant Government Department in the other country). The purpose of the application is to return your child to the UK so that the Courts here can make a decision about residence and contact.

The Child Abduction Unit will help you to locate an overseas lawyer and, depending on the legal aid system in the foreign country, it may not be necessary for you to pay your overseas lawyer. They will advise you on this.

What do I do if the children have been taken to a country that is not a signatory to the Hague Convention?

In the event that your child has been taken to a country that is not a signatory to the Hague or European agreements, then the Foreign and Commonwealth Office and its network of Embassies abroad are committed to providing advice and support.

The Foreign and Commonwealth Office can approach Interpol in the UK and other overseas authorities for help in tracing the child; put pressure on foreign Courts to handle a case more quickly; provide travel advice and assist with finding safe accommodation; draw the attention of overseas Courts to any UK Court Orders in force (with the UK Court's permission); provide a translation service for legal documents; in exceptional circumstances, attend Court hearings or visit the child to ensure they are safe.

5.3 DOMESTIC VIOLENCE

What does the term "domestic violence" actually mean?

Domestic violence is now commonly held to include physical violence, psychological abuse, emotional abuse and financial control. If you are a victim of domestic violence, you need seek help to protect yourself and your children from harm.

What does "harm" actually mean?

"Harm" means ill-treatment or the impairment of health or development. This can include impairment suffered from seeing or hearing the ill-treatment of another person. If children witness domestic violence, even when it isn't directed at them, the law considers that they are directly suffering.

"Development" (insofar as a child is concerned) includes a child's physical, intellectual, emotional, social and behavioural development. "Health" includes both physical and mental health. "Ill-treatment" includes sexual abuse and forms of ill-treatment that are not physical such as neglect.[95]

Why do people stay in an abusive relationship?

People stay in an abusive relationship for a number of reasons. A common reason is that the victim's self-esteem becomes reliant on the abuser's opinion. There may be fear of what the abuser will do if they tell anyone, there may be guilt or shame at being in the situation, a feeling of helplessness, a false feeling of responsibility for the abuse and a fear of how they will cope financially if they leave.

What are the effects on children of domestic violence?

Suffering abuse or witnessing domestic violence can have serious effects on children including ill health, anti-social behaviour, drug and alcohol abuse and self-harm. There can also be longer-term effects leading into adulthood. These can include anxiety, depression, substance abuse, eating disorders and self-destructive behaviour. Sustained abuse can also have a deep impact on the children's self-esteem and lead to difficulties forming relationships in later life, problems with employment and impact on their own parenting ability.

Who can provide advice and practical assistance?

Government agencies such as Social Services and the Police can provide practical help and support, as can charities that specialise in this area. This can include counselling, and the provision of a place of safety if required.

Has a crime been committed if my partner has hit my children?

Possibly, depending on why they hit your child, and how the child was hit. Individuals with parental responsibility have the legal right to use "reasonable" physical punishment to discipline their children.

It is illegal to punish children to the extent that they become a victim of battery, suffer grievous bodily harm, actual bodily harm or experience punishment that could be considered to be cruelty.[75]

Bodily harm includes any physical harm calculated to interfere with the health or comfort of the victim.

If you are unsure as to whether your partner's methods of punishment are excessive, you could contact the NSPCC to discuss this, if you had concerns about discussing it with your partner.

What will the Police do if I call them?

You should call the Police if you believe either you or your children are in danger, are being harassed, if your property has been damaged, you are being threatened, or have been physically assaulted. The Police have the power to enter any premises and arrest someone guilty of causing injury to another person or damage to property.[96]

The Police are often the first point of contact for families where domestic violence is taking place and have extensive powers to ensure your safety.

If the Police believe that the children are at risk of harm, and depending on the severity of the circumstances, the Police can:

- refer the matter to Social Services. This will be done if there are concerns about the children's safety or if the Officer believes that the children are suffering harm.
- secure the safety of the victims in their home. Where this isn't possible, the Police should take them to a place of safety, such as a relative's home or refuge accommodation.
- arrest the offender when a crime has been committed to ensure the safety of the victim while the offense is investigated. If there hasn't been physical violence, the Police can still remove the aggressive party from the property if they believe that it might be dangerous or result in a breach of the peace to leave them there.

Will someone be arrested if they are accused of domestic violence?

Some forms of domestic violence are criminal offences, for which the offender can be arrested and prosecuted, such as

- Common assault. This includes causing injury or putting the victim in fear of injury or causing injury.[97]
- Assault causing actual bodily harm.[98]
- Criminal damage to property.[99]
- Harassment. A charge of harassment can only be brought if harassment has occurred on two separate occasions but can include both physical and verbal conduct.[100]
- Rape or Indecent assault.[101]

Will the Police take domestic violence seriously?

Yes. A recent advertising campaign run by the Metropolitan Police sets out their views on domestic violence. "The Met is committed to holding domestic violence offenders accountable and we will arrest given reasonable grounds. We are no longer reliant upon the victim's statement to do this and will pursue abusers independently."[102]

I don't think I'm in immediate danger, what should I do?

Contact either the NSPCC or Social Services and explain your concerns. They will advise you on courses of action which can be taken and can provide practical assistance to ensure your children's safety and wellbeing.

Aren't parents who contact Social Services seen to be failing?

No. Social Services will view your request for support as a sign of your being a responsible, rather than an incapable, parent.

How can independent charities help me?

The Women's Aid Federation strives to end domestic violence against women and children. They provide practical advice and assistance. In addition, they have some 440 properties at the time of printing providing over 3400 rooms in shared houses. They also have an advice line for men who are victims of domestic violence.

Can a solicitor help me?

Yes. If you are experiencing domestic violence a solicitor can help you to apply for a number of different Court Orders to ensure your safety:

- An Emergency Protection Order (see Chapter 2.5) to remove temporarily your ex-partner from the property. This Order may be made if the children are considered to be at risk of significant harm.
- A Non-Molestation Order.[103] This Order can be made to protect an ex-partner or their child. The term molestation includes violence, pestering, harassment and threatening behaviour. A Non-Molestation Order can be made on an ex-parte basis.
- An Occupation Order.[104] This Order can be used in circumstances where the applicant had left the family home and subsequently

wished to return. An example of circumstances where the Order would be considered is where a partner had entered a refuge and then wished to return to the family home. An Occupation Order can provide for the exclusion of the abusive party.

To apply for an Occupation Order, you must either have an interest in the home property (e.g. the property being in joint names) or the property must be the matrimonial home.

Restrictions can be placed on your (ex)-partner setting out the penalties if these restrictions are broken (such as a stipulation that they may not visit the property, under the penalty of fines or, as a last resort, jail, for breaching the order).

I'm separated from my violent ex-partner but they want to see the children. Would the Court allow them to if they applied for a Contact Order?

The following statement by the President of the Family Division of the High Court provides an indication of what the Court should consider when assessing contact for a parent where there are allegations of domestic violence.

> "On an application for interim contact, when allegations of domestic violence have not yet been adjudicated upon, the Court should give particular consideration to the likely risk of harm to the child, whether physical or emotional, if contact is granted or refused. The Court should ensure, as far as it can, that any risk of harm to the child is minimised and the safety of the child and the residential parent is secured before, during and after any such contact."[105]

The Court will consider safety first when assessing whether contact should be allowed, and what form contact should take. Contact centres can be used to facilitate contact on a supervised basis.

It is important for children to have contact with both of their parents, but their safety will always be the Court's priority.

Is there help for abusers?

Yes. Respect is the UK membership association for domestic violence perpetrator programmes and support services. Their objective is to increase the safety of people experiencing domestic violence by promoting effective interventions.

Respect provides a telephone service offering information and advice to domestic violence perpetrators, their partner, ex-partner and friends and family.

If you are a perpetrator of domestic violence, the Court may take into account your willingness to recognise that you have a problem and are willing to get help.

5.4 SEXUAL ABUSE

What is sexual abuse?

Sexual abuse involves forcing or enticing a child to take part in sexual activities, whether or not the child is aware of what is happening to them. Sexual abuse need not be physical, and includes involving children in viewing pornographic material.

Can I handle this on my own?

This isn't something you should handle on your own, so get professional help and protect your children immediately.

You need support and advice and should contact either Social Services, the Police or the National Society for the Prevention of Cruelty to Children (NSPCC).

What can I do to help my children cope?

Firstly, ensure their protection. Refer to Chapter 5.3 about the ways in which the Police, Social Services and a solicitor can help you.

Your children will need reassurance that they are not responsible for the abuse and are in no way to blame. Tell them they have done the right thing in letting you know, that you believe what they say and act in a way which won't increase their distress.

You may be worried about your children being taken into care, but in most cases it is the child abuser who is removed from the family home.

5.5 MENTAL HEALTH PROBLEMS

What is a mental health problem?

From a legal standpoint, a mental health problem is an illness, disorder or impairment of the mind that includes either a significant or severe impairment of intelligence and social functioning resulting in abnormally aggressive or seriously irresponsible conduct.[106]

If my partner suffers from a mental health problem, will they be considered to be unfit to care for my children?

It depends on how the condition affects them and the severity of the illness or disorder. Having a mental health problem doesn't mean that the sufferer is either unsafe or incapable of being a competent parent, especially if the condition is treatable, manageable and the person is willing to engage in treatment.

What should I do if I think my children are in immediate danger?

If your partner is unwilling to seek help and you consider that your children are in immediate danger, contact Social Services to raise your concerns. If you are not separated from your partner (you still live together) you could consider a request that they be assessed under the Mental Health Act (see Chapter 5.6).

If you are separated, you can still contact Social Services who have a duty to investigate if they have reasonable cause to suspect that children who live in their area are suffering, or likely to suffer, significant harm.[37]

Is there anything else I should do if I contact Social Services?

Yes. Social Services' priority won't be to return your children to you, but to ensure their safety.

If Social Services share your concerns and subsequently apply to the Court for a Care Order, you will only be automatically involved in decisions about who would look after your children if you have Parental Responsibility for them. Read Chapter 3.1 to see if you have Parental Responsibility, and, if not, you should seek immediate legal advice.

Could I apply through the Court to protect my children?

Yes. You can approach a solicitor and ask that they apply for an Emergency Protection Order to ensure your children's safety (see Chapter 2.5). At this point you could also apply for a Residence Order and ask the Court to consider ordering that a forensic psychological assessment be carried out on your ex-partner.

As the applicant for an Emergency Protection Order, if the Court shared your concern and granted the Order, the children would be returned to you. A Residence Order automatically grants Parental Responsibility to the applicant.

What do I do if I consider the relationship to be over, but my children aren't in immediate danger?

Apply to the Court for a Residence Order and raise your concerns in your statement to the Court. You should also ensure that your solicitor request that a forensic psychological assessment be carried out (see Chapter 4.3) to determine the nature and extent of any risk to your children.

What should I tell the Court?

When writing your statement for the Court, include details of your partner's behaviour and how you believe it affects their ability to care for your children and ensure their safety.

You should also include the frequency with which events happens. Include dates if you can and statements from other people who have witnessed incidents that concern you.

What behaviour could indicate my ex-partner has a mental health problem?

The following behaviour may indicate your ex-partner has a mental health problem:

Depressive symptoms and behaviour: addiction problems, anger, anxiety, changes in eating patterns, difficulty concentrating, difficulty making decisions, empty feelings, forgetfulness, inappropriate guilt, irritability, lack of energy, negative thinking, poor confidence, poor motivation, poor self-esteem, problems sleeping (too much or too little), reduced interest in activities, relationship difficulties, social isolation, staying in bed, suicidal thoughts, vague and frequent physical complaints and withdrawal from friends and family.

To qualify as an illness or disorder, many of these symptoms will need to have been persistent (long term) and pervasive (affecting the person for much of the time).

Manic symptoms and behaviour: aggression, anger, euphoria, excessive laughter, extravagance, hyperactivity, increased appetite, increased sex drive, overconfidence, pressured speech, and reduced need for sleep. Risk-taking or reckless behaviour such as spending sprees, speeding and dangerous driving.

People experiencing a manic episode can appear to be great fun and exciting to people who are ignorant of the condition.

Acute anxiety: cold hands and feet, dizziness, feelings of fear, muscle tension, perspiration, rapid heart rate, restlessness, shortness of breath and trembling.

Delusional thoughts: paranoia (an irrational belief that people are plotting against them or dislike them), severe hypochondria e.g. a healthy person believing they have a terminal illness and grandiose belief (exaggerated ideas of importance or identity).

Delusion is a confusion between reality and fantasy. Delusional thoughts are those that are false, unusual and are firmly held. The belief must not be an "ordinary" belief within the person's culture or religion.

Other: eating disorders, hallucinations (sensory perceptions such as hearing, seeing, feeling and smelling something that isn't there), memory problems (disorientation or confusion), obsessions (recurrent and persistent thoughts and impulses), repetitive behaviour (including compulsions such as repetitive hand washing) and self-harming behaviour (such as cutting one's skin).

Bear in mind that if your ex-partner was unhappy in the relationship, some of these behaviours could be entirely normal in those circumstances. When discussing your partner's mental health with the Court or any agency carrying out an assessment, don't suggest what the illness could be, but keep your conversation to the behaviour that concerns you (unless your partner has a medical diagnosis).

Let the assessor diagnose and determine what is wrong with your partner. Assist them in their diagnosis by presenting them with a history and your observations and experiences.

What other factors could be relevant to assist the assessor?

There are a number of factors that can be relevant and assist in diagnosis. If you are aware of any of the factors listed below, ensure that the assessor is made aware of them:

1. Does any other member of your partner's family have a mental health condition or a history of mental illness/disorder?
2. Did your partner suffer psychological, emotional, sexual, or physical abuse as a child?
3. Did your partner suffer from neglect as a child?
4. Detail any traumatic events that your partner has suffered such as bereavement, abortion, assault, and accidents including trauma to the head.
5. Has your partner ever had dealings with mental health services or counselling services?
6. Has your partner ever attempted suicide or "self-harmed"?
7. What is your partner's employment record like?
8. Did your partner experience problems at school?
9. Has your partner ever had addiction problems (either alcohol or drug-related, gambling, shopping, or sex-related).
10. What is your ex-partner's relationship like with their birth family (parents and siblings)?
11. Does your partner have any previous convictions (including

speeding fines or endorsements that could be symptomatic of manic behaviour)?

None of these factors necessarily lead to a diagnosis of mental illness or personality disorder, however, they form a part of a picture, and certain illnesses and disorders have these as possible causative factors or indicators.

What should an assessment include?

Ideally, the assessment should be conducted over time, with more than one face-to-face meeting between your ex-partner and the psychologist.

Psychopathic disorders can feature "denial" of the disorder as a symptom. When a parent's involvement with their children can be affected by the outcome of the assessment, co-operation and honesty can understandably be reduced. Also, a single assessment can be a matter of "pot luck" depending on how the person appears on the day. Variation of thought and behaviour can be typical of conditions such as bi-polar disorder (manic depression), borderline personality disorder and cyclothymia, and for these, a single assessment meeting may not allow diagnosis.

What questions should an assessment answer?

The psychologist's report should clearly answer whether your ex-partner has a mental health problem or not. If there is a problem, the psychologist should express an opinion on the questions detailed on the following page (with their opinion included in their report for the Court):

a)   What is the psychologist's opinion of the likelihood of successful treatment?

b) Did the psychologist have sufficient time to diagnose, and do they feel that further assessment is warranted?

c) Does the psychologist have an opinion as to the timescale for treatment being effective?

d) Is the condition manageable by medication?

e) How quickly could the condition improve through the use of medication?

f) What is the availability of any treatment that may assist your ex-partner and are there waiting lists for services?

g) To what extent is the condition exacerbated by the current exceptional stresses of the Court case and has the psychologist considered this in their assessment?

h) Does the psychologist believe that the condition presents risks to the children or affects your ex-partner's ability to provide your children with adequate care?

i) What are the risks?

j) If there are risks, can these risks be minimised or eliminated with treatment and support?

If the psychologist hasn't considered these points in their report, it may leave them open to a successful challenge from your ex-partner's barrister. The Court will then be left with the difficult decision of either asking for further assessments to be carried out or having to base its judgment on the incomplete information before them.

If you can, ensure that your solicitor asks that the above questions be included in the instructions to the psychologist before the assessment is started. This should reduce the possibility of further assessments being required and the final judgment being delayed.

5.6 ASSESSMENT UNDER SECTION 2 OF THE MENTAL HEALTH ACT 1983

When will Social Services consider making an application for an Assessment under the Mental Health Act?[107]

When it is believed that someone is affected by a mental health problem to the extent that they may be a risk to themselves or others.

Who manages the application?

An Approved Social Worker working for Social Services, who has received training to assist them in dealing with people who are suffering from a mental disorder.[108] They will also have detailed knowledge of the local mental health services that are available.

What will the Approved Social Worker do?

They will consider the information that is presented to them. If they have concerns, they will make arrangements for the person to be seen by two doctors, one of which has "special experience in the diagnosis or treatment of mental disorder" and, if practically possible, the other having had "previous acquaintance" with the person being assessed (e.g. the person's General Practitioner).

When would the person be detained in hospital?

The grounds for the application for an assessment must be that the doctors who saw the person believe:

1. The person is suffering from mental disorder of a nature or degree which warrants the detention of the patient in a hospital for assessment (or for assessment followed by medical treatment) for at least a limited period; and

2. They ought to be so detained in the interests of their own health or safety or with a view to the protection of other persons.

How long could the person be detained for under this application?

28 days.

What happens then?

The person can be detained for treatment for up to six months if:[109]

1. They are suffering from mental illness, severe mental impairment, psychopathic disorder, or mental impairment and their mental disorder is of a nature or degree which make it appropriate for the patient to receive medical treatment in a hospital; and

2. In the case of psychopathic disorder or mental impairment, such treatment is likely to alleviate or prevent a deterioration of their condition; and

3. It is necessary for the health or safety of the patient or for the protection of other persons that they should receive such treatment and it cannot be provided unless they are detained.

Can I request that my ex-partner be assessed under the Mental Health Act?

It depends on your living circumstances. You can't make the application if you are permanently separated from your partner or if you deserted them.

You can apply if you are not separated, have been co-habiting for at least six months or are married to them.

If you are not living with your partner, while you can't apply yourself, you could contact Social Services and ask to speak to an Approved Social Worker. Raise your concerns with them, and they may decide to make the application themselves.

If you are disqualified from applying due to being separated, your ex-partner's next 'nearest relative' could also apply. In all cases, the nearest relative must have seen the person who is going to be assessed within the last 14 days.

What is a 'nearest relative'?

For a person to be considered the nearest relative, they must be over the age of 18, a resident of the United Kingdom (including the Channel Islands and Isle of Man) and (in order of priority) the:

1. Husband or Wife (unless permanently separated)
2. Son or Daughter
3. Father or Mother
4. Brother or Sister
5. Grandparent
6. Grandchild
7. Uncle or Aunt
8. Nephew or Niece
9. Someone, not a relative, with whom the person concerned normally resides, and has done so for at least five years

How should an application be made?

Ideally, the application should be made in writing and sent by registered post or hand delivered to Social Services if the situation is an emergency. The letter should specifically state:

- that the person applying is the nearest relative
- that they are applying for a Section 2 Assessment under the Mental Health Act 1983
- the reasons for the application (with supporting evidence)
- details of any previous diagnosis or treatment of which the applicant is aware
- that the applicant has seen the person to be assessed within the last 14 days.

What happens then?

The Act allows the person to be detained in hospital for assessment, although the person being assessed will only be detained if the doctors carrying out the assessment believe it to be necessary.

If the person is detained in hospital, a Responsible Medical Officer (RMO) will keep the need for detention in hospital under constant review and end the detention when it is no longer required. The patient will have the right to appeal against their detention to the Mental Health Act Managers.

What other rights does the nearest relative have?

The nearest relative has the power to discharge the person being assessed but they have to give the Mental Health Act Managers 72 hours notice in writing.[110]

Is there anything else that I should consider?

Yes. An assessment under the Mental Health Act ensures that a person with a mental disorder is assessed and detained when they are considered to be a risk to themselves or others. It doesn't address the matter of who should look after the children while the person is detained.

If your children live with you and you have Parental Responsibility for them, or if you have a Joint Residence Order, this shouldn't be an issue while your (ex)-partner receives treatment.

My children don't normally live with me, what should I do?

If you have Parental Responsibility for your children but they normally live with your ex-partner, or your ex-partner has a Residence Order stating that the children live with them, they won't automatically come to live with you.

If you have Parental Responsibility, Social Services and the Court should automatically include you in discussions about where the children should live if Social Services apply for a Care Order to resolve this issue.

I don't have Parental Responsibility, what should I do?

Seek immediate legal advice. Depending on the circumstances, you may decide that it is appropriate for you to apply to the Court to have any existing Residence Order changed in your favour.

If there is no Residence Order in force, you could apply for a Residence Order. If a Court grants your residence, this would automatically give you Parental Responsibility for the children.

If you decide not to alter or apply for residence, you should consider applying for a Parental Responsibility Order to ensure that you are involved in decisions about your children's future (refer to Chapter 3.1).

5.7 FALSE ALLEGATIONS

Why do people make false allegations?

1. Your ex-partner may be motivated by anger, jealousy or revenge.
2. Some people, having decided their relationship is over, want their ex-partner permanently out of their life and the lives of their children.
3. There may be underlying mental health reasons which can affect their anxiety in relation to their child and fears about their partner.
4. Your ex-partner may have been advised that they are a victim of domestic violence for behaviour which a Court may not consider to fall under such a serious classification.

Some victim support organisations consider behaviour which can be common in a relationship under strain within their classification of domestic violence. Examples include disrespect, interrupting telephone calls, not listening or responding when talked to, lying, being jealous, breaking promises or sulking. While such behaviour is clearly wrong, a label of domestic violence may be inappropriate.

While the allegations may be unfounded, it doesn't mean that your ex-partner is not genuinely fearful. Try to bear this in mind. Facing any allegation is painful, and an allegation that someone thinks your child could suffer harm while in your care can be incredibly hurtful. If the Court decides the allegation needs to be investigated, that is all it is, a decision to investigate.

How could a false allegation affect me?

When an allegation is made against you that suggests potential for harm to either your children or your ex-partner, the Court needs to ensure their safety. The Court can make a number of different Orders to protect the alleged victims while allegations are investigated. These powers are discussed in Chapter 5.3.

While an investigation into the allegations is conducted, the Court may make interim orders that give residence to your ex-partner, force you to leave the family home or only allow you limited contact with your children. In these circumstances your ex-partner will be the main carer for the children while the investigations are carried out.

In the above circumstances, the status quo will build in your ex-partner's favour. At the Final Hearing, the Court may decide that your partner should continue to look after your children since a further change to their living situation would cause them too much disruption.

What should I do if I'm falsely accused?

For any serious allegation, you should:

- seek legal advice.
- consider the motives and reasons for the allegations and whether these could result from a mental illness on the part of the accuser. In these circumstances consider applying for your ex-partner to undergo a psychological assessment.
- have your solicitor clarify the precise details of the allegation.

If the allegation is "domestic violence", what are you actually accused of?

- consider the evidence that your ex-partner may have to support the allegation.

- have your solicitor apply to the Court and present evidence (if you have any) which proves your innocence.

- ask for the allegation to be fully investigated by qualified professionals.

- refer to Chapter 4.4 on Tips for Assessment interviews.

- request an Interim Contact Order (if your partner is granted interim residence) while any investigations are carried out. If necessary, agree to supervised contact to maintain contact with your children.

Don't ignore serious allegations. In Family Law, Court judgments are based on 'a balance of probabilities' rather than on firm evidence.

What do I do if I'm accused of domestic violence?

If there is no evidence to support the allegation, point this out clearly to the Court. You could ask the Court to have Social Services or CAFCASS carry out an investigation. Refer to Chapter 4.1 and 4.2. Statements from friends and family in support of your character may help.

What do I do if I'm accused of being mentally ill?

If you have never been diagnosed with a mental illness or received treatment, make the Court aware of this. If necessary, volunteer for a psychological evaluation and have a Forensic Psychologist carry out the investigation. If you don't qualify for legal aid, ask that your ex-partner either pay for this, or that the costs be shared.

A cheaper alternative is to have your GP provide your solicitor with a written medical opinion. Be aware that your ex-partner's solicitor may challenge whether a GP is sufficiently qualified to make a diagnosis of mental illness or personality disorder.

What do I do if I'm accused of being a drug addict?

If you're accused of drug addiction, consider paying for a forensic drug test to prove your innocence. A solicitor can arrange this and request that the test be based on hair samples.

Hair records a history of drug use over a far longer period than urine or blood. Each centimetre of hair growth records roughly one month of drug abuse history. For the purpose of the test, hair samples can be taken from any part of the body.

What do I do if I'm accused of denigrating my ex-partner's character?

Ask if there are written statements provided by the people to whom you are accused of speaking.

If these statements support your ex-partner's allegation, ask for the people to be called as witnesses. If the Court agrees, the witnesses can be challenged and cross-examined by your solicitor or barrister.

What do I do if I'm accused of child abuse?

Speak to your solicitor about requesting an independent child psychologist to interview your children. You will need the Court's permission for this. The Police and CAFCASS or Social Services are likely to be involved in any investigation.

What do I do if I'm accused of neglect or poor parenting skills?

If you face an allegation of poor parenting ability, consider who you could ask for statements confirming that you are a capable parent. A report from the Health Visitor (for babies and toddlers), playgroup, General Practitioner, school reports, and statements from friends and family may be of assistance. If CAFCASS carry out an investigation, suggest they contact these people to gain opinions on your parenting ability.

If you have been the children's primary carer, question why these allegations are being made now? The Court should also consider this.

When presenting your ability to provide adequate care, set out how your children's health, stage of development, behaviour and involvement in outside activities compares to that of their peers.

What is Parental Alienation Syndrome?

You may have heard of Parental Alienation Syndrome and believe it has some relevance. It doesn't. This term is used in American Family Law and psychology, and while some lay people may use it in the United Kingdom, it is not officially recognised.

Parental Alienation Syndrome is where one parent deliberately seeks to turn children against the other parent, and to convince them that the non-resident parent is abusive, violent, or simply a "bad" person. While this behaviour is seen in England and Wales, it isn't believed to be a psychological syndrome, but an example of one parent's "implacable hostility" to the other.

Will the Court punish my ex-partner for making false allegations?

The Courts are unlikely to penalise someone for making false allegations, but will take their behaviour and honesty into consideration. Each allegation you are able to disprove can count in your favour.

People wanting the best for their children don't falsely accuse the other parent of negligence, criminal offences or mental health problems. Unfounded allegations of abuse are often disproved and damage the credibility of the person making them. An example of one such case is given below:

> The Judge "found that the mother had caused the children to believe that they had suffered abuse at the hands of the father and paternal grandparents, and that an assessment was needed when the children were not at home with the mother. This was secured away from the home under an interim care order. Free from the mother's influence, the children were rapidly able to re-establish their relationship with the father. Subsequently an Order was made that they reside with him. Although this approach is not appropriate in all cases involving disputing parents, it is a useful tool to have available. If it is clear that contact is desirable but one parent obstructs it, the risk of significant harm may be present." [111]

5.8 UPHELD ALLEGATIONS

What should I do if allegations against me are considered to be true by an expert witness?

An expert witness would potentially be CAFCASS, Social Services, a Psychologist etc. Firstly, consider their findings. If you don't agree with them, you should:

1. Challenge the basis upon which the professional expressed their opinion.

2. Determine whether the expert's opinion or report includes any statements which are ambiguous, confused, open to misinterpretation or contradictory.

3. Consider if the expert is expressing an opinion or making a statement of fact (e.g. presenting the results of a drug test).

4. Determine if the expert is qualified to provide an opinion on the subject (e.g. in the case of a CAFCASS Officer believing you had mental health problems, you could challenge whether they are medically qualified to do so).

5. Consider any evidence which supports the expert's opinion.

6. Consider any evidence which supports your belief that the allegation is untrue.

7. Consider whether the expert has acted within the instructions which were originally made by the Court.

8. Find out if the expert has adhered to their professional guidelines.

9. Discuss the matter with your solicitor, and consider retaining the services of a barrister who is experienced in cross-examining expert witnesses and challenging what they say.

What do I do if the allegations are true?

Admit to them and address them.

If you have drug or alcohol problems, speak with your General Practitioner and ask about, and sign up to, a treatment programme. If you can demonstrate to the Court that you admit to having a problem, and are committed to dealing with it, they will take this into consideration.

Similarly, if you have been guilty of domestic violence, a willingness to address problems with anger management may help and will certainly be in your children's best interests.

I have a history of mental health problems, what should I do?

If there is historic evidence of mental illness, the key point is just that, it's historic. Have your solicitor challenge the relevance of this, and be prepared to volunteer for a current psychological assessment. There will be a cost for assessment, and your solicitor can suggest to the Court that your ex-partner pays for this. If you have legal aid, this may cover the cost. If you are seeing a therapist, would they be prepared to write a report for the Court?

I've had a psychological assessment that indicates that I have mental health problems, what should I do?

Check whether the psychologist's report addresses the following questions. If it doesn't, your barrister should raise the following questions in Court.

1. What is the psychologist's opinion of the likelihood of successful treatment, given your willingness to participate?

2. Does the psychologist have an opinion as to the timescale for treatment being effective?

3. Is the condition manageable by medication?

4. How quickly could the condition improve through the use of medication?

5. What is the availability of any treatment that may assist you and are there waiting lists for services?

6. To what extent is the condition exacerbated by the current exceptional stresses of the Court case and have they considered this in their assessment?

7. Does the psychologist believe that the condition presents risk to the children or affects your ability to provide them with adequate care?

8. If there are risks, can these risks be minimised or eliminated with treatment and support?

Other questions that you need the Court to consider include:

1. What evidence exists to support the argument that you're not capable, or less capable, of looking after your child than your ex-partner?

2. What evidence is available which supports you in proving you are a capable parent?

3. If you've always been the main carer for your child, what justification is there to support the opinion that you are now incapable, especially if your ex-partner has previously been happy to leave you alone with the children?

If you accept the psychologist's opinion, and are proactive in engaging the support of Social Services and the Mental Health Trust, and are undergoing treatment, this will count in your favour. The Court is concerned about the best interests of the child, and any decision it takes will be based on this, taking into account all of your and your ex-partner's circumstances, not just those relating to mental health.

Consider contacting MIND, the main UK charity for mental health, which has a Legal Unit providing advice and information. Remember that mental illness can affect anyone.

What information could help show you're a capable parent?

Any information you can gather which shows that your children are unaffected by your condition will assist you. Consider having your solicitor request the following reports and present them to the Court as evidence supporting your capability as a parent:

- Health Visitor Report: if you have a child under school age, ask for a report from the health visitor commenting on your child's general state of care, stage of development, and if they have had any concerns.

- Playgroup/Nursery Reports: these can be used to show whether your child is showing age appropriate development and behaviour, and can again act to reassure the Court.

- School Reports: if your child's behaviour is fine, and stage of development and achievement gives no cause for concern, this can support you.

- A letter from your General Practitioner confirming there have been no problems.

- Statements from any other third party professional who sees your child or has witnessed your parenting.

- Statements from friends and family confirming that you have a good support network around you.

What do I do if assessments conclude that there is risk to my children?

If it is found that your condition or behaviour does pose significant risks to your child, you may need to accept that while you receive treatment, it is best for your child that your ex-partner be the main carer.

Talk with your solicitor about the possibility of assessment in the future following treatment and recovery. You could consider reapplying to the Court to review its decision once "risk" is no longer a concern. Have your solicitor ask the Court to consider supervised contact until such time as supervision is no longer required.

5.9 STRESS AND EMOTIONS

What stresses do people normally experience when separating?

Separation and Family Law cases include many stress factors. These can include (and this is in no way an exhaustive list):

- grieving and guilt over the demise of your relationship and a sense of failure
- worrying whether your children will live with you or not
- not knowing how often you will be allowed to see your children
- being concerned and hurt over allegations
- feeling excluded from important decisions about your children's lives
- worrying about your finances
- feeling lonely
- feeling you have little control over what is going to happen
- having to arrange new accommodation.

Feelings of stress arise when situations feel outside our control. Being stressed in these circumstances is entirely natural and appropriate to the situation.

How can I cope with these stresses?

If you find everything is getting too much, sit down with a close family member or a counsellor and prioritise what you need to do. You may decide that work will have to suffer and perhaps you need some time off for stress. Speak to your GP.

Again, use telephone helplines if you need to - it's what they're there for. They are staffed by caring people. The Samaritans operate 24 hours a day. They may have other advice on what you can do to help reduce some of your stress. While you cannot remove yourself from this situation, you do have to get through it, so try to make it manageable.

If you find yourself venting at your solicitor, remember it costs upwards of £150 an hour to talk to them, while a counsellor costs £35 an hour and is better qualified to help you cope emotionally. You can find a local private counsellor by contacting the British Association for Counselling and Psychotherapy or by being referred by your General Practitioner.

Accept that you are only human, and don't be embarrassed by asking for help.

My work is suffering and my employer is unsupportive, what can I do?

In some ways, it's better to take time out, rather than struggle on at work when you're not hitting targets or reaching the required level of performance. Your health is important for both yourself and your children.

Ensure your employer is aware of the difficulties you are experiencing. Speak to your General Practitioner and consider being signed off work due to stress.

If you have been suffering from stress for more than twelve months, legally this could count as a disability, further strengthening your legal rights. Contact the Disability Rights Commission who will be able to advise you.

My ex-partner keeps trying to start an argument, what should I do?

If anything contentious comes up while talking to your ex-partner, refuse to discuss it immediately by saying you want to think about what they have said. Agree to write to them, or ask them to write to you. This gives you time to consider what you say, and have someone else check your reply. Ideally, have your solicitor read, edit, and then send the letter on your behalf.

Arguments with your ex-partner won't make the situation better, and are likely to put you in a much weaker position.

What if I want the Court to see how badly my ex-partner has behaved?

The Court will respect you if you keep your concerns objective while the case is proceeding (and afterwards) and will take note of your behaviour. Keep statements to the Court unemotional and factual, and concentrate on concerns about your children and their relationship with you.

What if I want my children to know I'm not the 'bad' party?

Disparaging your ex-partner to your children will cause them emotional harm. By all means speak to a close family member about how dreadful your ex-partner is if you need to, but it isn't appropriate to say this to your children.

Be aware that discussing the details of the case with friends is not allowed in law (see Chapter 1.9). To help you to cope with the emotional stresses of the Court Case, the law allows you to discuss details of the case with a close family member or a counsellor.[10]

Your children will make up their own minds and who is at fault matters less than how your children are cared for. Be a loving and capable parent and this will be how they perceive you to be.

What else can I do?

Humour and laughter help to relieve stress so see the irony in situations where you can. Letting out pent-up emotion reduces feelings of stress, so don't be afraid to cry. Find places where you can let out emotions safely, and with people who will be supportive.

Try to have some activities that take you away from the situation. Don't feel guilty about going out with friends and having some fun if you feel able to.

Stress can take its toll on you physically, so ensure you eat healthily and get plenty of sleep. Taking part in sport will also help since exercise stimulates the production of endorphins and natural opiates that help to create a sense of well-being. Sport can also help with self-esteem and act as a distraction from the Court case.

Are there things I shouldn't do?

Don't turn to drink and cut down on the caffeine in your diet. Both of these can increase feelings of anxiety.

Will everyone understand my stress?

Not necessarily. You need to consider how you are perceived.

- If you lose your temper with an assessor, Social Services, CAFCASS, or in front of the Judge, you may be accused of being an "aggressive character".

- If you appear overly emotional, you may be accused of being an anxious person.

- If you lose your temper with your ex-partner, you may be accused of domestic violence (which includes emotional/psychological and physical abuse).

Don't expect people to make allowances for you. Consider your behaviour in front of anyone who may report back to the Court.

Remember what is at stake, and take the steps you need to help you to cope. Your children need you to be balanced, stable, and healthy. They also need you to get through this in one piece, and you need to not only be a reasonable person, but you need to be seen to be a reasonable person.

5.10 HELPING YOUR CHILDREN COPE

How can I help my children to cope with the separation?

You children will be affected by your separation. The way in which you behave with your ex-partner, the amount of reassurance you give your children, and how you behave in front of the children will either increase or reduce their stress. Ensure conversations are appropriate to their age and emotional development.

How will your children react and how can you help?

No two children will necessarily react in the same way, but all will have underlying worries and thoughts that you need to be aware of, and to help them to handle.

Guilt

Reassure your child that they are in no way to blame or responsible for the situation. Regardless of their age, perhaps the best way to let them know about the divorce is to say "Mummy and Daddy have decided not to be together and will be happier living apart." If both of you can tell your children together, this will help.

Insecurity

Your children need to be reassured as to what will happen to them, where they will live, and that they won't "lose" one of their parents. Most importantly, they need to be reassured that both parents unconditionally love them.

When younger children see their parents separate, they may believe or fear that their parents' love for them is also conditional and uncertain. Reassure your children that both parents love them and will always be there for them.

Change

Change brings about insecurity. Keep to established routines. If the children are used to seeing grandparents at a certain time, keep to this. If they have set activities, ensure they are maintained.

With regard to contact, establish new routines as quickly as you can. Speak with your ex-partner and keep to the same bedtime routines, rules, methods of discipline, and ensure you work collaboratively in their upbringing. Don't try to outbid each other with treats and toys since your children need consistency, and most importantly, your time, security and love. Expensive toys are a poor substitute.

It is also understandable, especially as the contact parent, to relax boundaries (such as disciplining your children for bad behaviour) since you don't want to risk your children being upset when they come to see you. Boundaries help children to feel secure and you can reduce your worry by strengthening the relationship with your children.

Confusion

Why is this happening? Give your children plenty of opportunities to ask questions, and limit your answers to give them enough to let them know what is going to happen, but not enough to disturb them. They don't need to know the details of the Court case, and hearing negative comments about their other parent will cause them distress. Keep feelings of anger and blame out of discussions. Let your child know that they can talk to you about how they feel at any time.

Sadness and Anger

Validate their feelings. "I know how sad/angry this has made you feel" and reassure them. "It will take a little time for all of us to get used to the change, but we both love you, and will always be there for you." Encourage them to talk about their feelings, and most importantly, listen to them.

Ask what would help them. It may be a phone call to their absent parent or knowing what is going to happen. You won't know unless you ask, and the very fact of being asked will help. Be as honest as you can about what will happen.

If there is a new partner in your life, you may face resentment since displaying affection for your new girlfriend or boyfriend can make your children feel disloyal or jealous. Accept that it will take time to adjust to a new situation. Ensure you spend time with them on your own and encourage them to talk about how they feel, and also talk about how you feel. Keep the conversation appropriate to their age and do not be disparage their other parent.

How can I strengthen my relationship with my children?

You strengthen your relationship by spending quality time together, when you can both relax and have fun. Find activities you both enjoy. For younger children, this could be going swimming, bowling, reading stories, taking them to activities and staying involved, playing games together, or going to watch them take part in activities (depending on their age).

Regardless of age, show an interest in what interests them. If you don't know, then now is the best time to ask.

Mix with friends and family who also have children, so there is an extended network of friends for them to play with and talk to when they are with you.

Keep your promises. If you say you will be there to pick them up at a certain time, or will take them out for the weekend, don't let them down. If you're not sure whether you'll be able to do something, don't promise it.

Keeping to age-appropriate rules and boundaries helps a child to feel secure and helps them prepare for life. Judge the times when those rules need to be relaxed a little, but if your children's behaviour slips, consider your own actions, and whether more attention needs to be paid to reassuring them by showing your love, interest, approval, and praise.

What warning signs of stress should I look out for? What should I do?

With toddlers and preschool children, watch for regressive behaviour such as thumb-sucking, bed-wetting and restless nights. They may become more sensitive, have tantrums, and engage in power struggles. Keep boundaries in place, but ensure they have your attention and reassurance.

With children of school age it is worthwhile letting the school know about the situation at home. If problems arise at school with the children's work or behaviour, then the school should be more sympathetic and can work with you to support your child rather than simply punishing them.

With teenagers, they may become more argumentative or withdrawn and you may notice other marked changes in their behaviour and attitude. Crisis situations could include running away, alcohol or drug problems, eating disorders, self-harm or depression. Don't be afraid to ask for outside help. Don't expect your children to adjust to the change overnight and give them time to heal. If you notice them emotionally supporting you through this change, think very carefully whether you should be seeking support from elsewhere. It isn't healthy for children to take on the role of parent and comforter.

If you become worried about the levels of stress your child is showing, then consider talking to your GP or a counsellor. Discuss your concerns with your ex-partner and work with them. If you can, encourage another member of your family such as your own siblings or parents or an adult family friend to let your child know they can talk to them. Choose someone who understands that blaming your ex-partner won't help the children.

Should I treat a teenager differently to a younger child?

Yes. Involve them in decisions about contact. This means you should include them in decisions about holidays and changing arrangements, but not necessarily agree to whatever they say.

What can I do if my children won't talk to me?

If they won't talk to you, and you are worried about how they are coping, consider giving them the telephone number of ChildLine or show them the website.

Reassure your children that you are always there to talk to them, but if they feel unable to confide in you, they can speak to someone at ChildLine and that what they say will be treated in confidence. It is better that they talk to a trained counsellor than bottle up their feelings.

Whatever your children's age, you can talk to your GP if you have concerns. Parentline Plus is an excellent organisation that provides support to parents and I would recommend talking to them if you need to. There is also a discussion forum on the Custody Minefield website where parents can exchange advice.

What shouldn't I do?

No matter the provocation, don't ever fight or argue with your ex-partner in front of your children. They learn from watching their parents, and in addition to the emotional harm caused by witnessing your arguments, it can cause problems that persist through to adulthood. Remember, the definition of harm to children within Family Law includes the impairment of a child's development resulting from seeing or hearing the ill treatment of another person.[95]

Children adjust most quickly to parental separation when their parents work collaboratively in their upbringing, and remain civil.

GLOSSARY

Advocate: Someone who speaks on your behalf. In a Court context, this would normally be your solicitor or a barrister.

Applicant: If you are applying for the Court to make a decision, the Court will refer to you as the Applicant.

Approved Social Worker: A Social Worker that is approved by the local authority as having appropriate competence and training relating to mental health issues. Under Section 114 of the Mental Health Act 1983 a local authority has an obligation to appoint a sufficient number of approved Social Workers described in the Act.

CAFCASS: The Children and Family Court Advisory and Support Service. Judges can request CAFCASS involvement, either to assist mediation between parents, or to carry out assessments of the family's circumstances.

Contact Parent: The parent in whose favour a Contact Order is made.

Custody: The old legal term for the parent who has their child living with them (for the majority of the time). This is now called Residence following the introduction of the Children Act 1989 which replaced previous legislation.

Data Controller: A person in an organisation tasked with ensuring the organisation complies with the Data Protection Act 1998.

Data Subject: A person on whom an organisation holds information and who has certain rights to that information, and how it's treated, under the

Data Protection Act 1998.

Direct Contact: Face-to-face contact, including visiting, staying and supervised contact (contact with a third party present or taking place in a Contact Centre).

Disposable Capital: In simple terms, what you're worth financially. Your disposable capital is calculated by taking the value of assets you own such as equity in your property, investments, savings etc and deducting any liabilities such as loans, your mortgage (the maximum deductible is £100,000).

Domestic Violence: A term which now commonly includes physical, emotional, psychological, or financial abuse and control.

Ex-Parte: Without the other party present (Applicant and Respondent in relation to Court hearings).

Forensic: Forensic means involved in the legal system and the Courts.

Gillick Principle: The principle that at a certain age, a child is sufficiently developed to make decisions which affects their own life.

Hague Convention: The Hague Convention on the Civil Aspects of International Child Abduction is an agreement made in October 1980 that covers the return of children taken from one member country to another.

Indirect Contact: Contact via telephone and correspondence.

Inter-Parte: With both parties present (Applicant and Respondent in relation to Court hearings).

Matrimonial Home: The main residence of a married couple.

McKenzie Friend: A person granted permission by the Court to assist you in Court and give advice, take notes etc. You are also permitted to share details of your case with a McKenzie Friend.

No Order Principle: The principle the Court adheres to, that an order will only be made if necessary.

Parental Alienation Syndrome: An American term, when one parent has caused their child to express at best complete indifference or, at worst, hatred towards the other parent. This isn't officially recognised as a "syndrome" in the UK, and such behaviour is normally referred to as implacable hostility.

Personality Inventory: A form of psychological test designed to identify mental disorders and personality traits.

Non-Resident Parent: The parent with whom the child doesn't reside. Usually, the non-resident parent is also the contact parent.

Rebuttal presumption: When it is presumed that something is held to be true unless someone comes forward to prove otherwise.

Resident Parent: The parent in whose favour a Residence Order is made.

Respondent: The person defending against an application being made is referred to as the Respondent.

Section 7 Report: A report prepared by Social Services for the Court, usually in circumstances where they have previously had an involvement with the family.

Section 8 Order: A Court Order made under Section 8 of the Children Act 1989 including Residence Orders, Contact Orders, Prohibited Steps Orders, and Specific Issue Orders.

Status Quo: The current situation.

Staying Contact: Children stay overnight with the non-resident parent.

SOURCES

Legislation

Access to Health Records Act 1990 [Crown Copyright 1990].

Adoption and Children Act 2002 [Crown Copyright 2002].

The Children Act 1989 [Crown Copyright 1989].

The Children Act 2004 [Crown Copyright 2004].

The Criminal Justice and Court Services Act 2000 [Crown Copyright 2000].

The Criminal Justice Act 1998 [Crown Copyright 1998].

The Data Protection Act 1998 [Crown Copyright 1998].

The Daycare and Child Minding (National Standards) (England) Regulations 2003 [Crown Copyright 2003].

The Education Act 1996 [Crown Copyright 1996].

The Education (Pupil Information) (England) Regulations 2005 [Crown Copyright 2005].

The Education (Pupil Information) (Wales) Regulations 2004 [Crown Copyright 2004].

The Emergency Protection Order (Transfer of Responsibilities) Regulations 1991 [Crown Copyright 1991].

The Family Law Act 1996 [Crown Copyright 1996].

The Family Proceedings (Amendment No 4) Rules 2005 [Crown Copyright 2005].

The Family Proceedings Courts (Miscellaneous Amendments) Rules 2005 [Crown Copyright 2005].

The Family Proceedings Rules 1991 [Crown Copyright 1991].

The Hague Convention on the Civil Aspects of International Child Abduction 1980.

The Human Rights Act 1998 [Crown Copyright 1998].

The Magistrates' Courts Act 1980 [Crown Copyright 1980].

The Mental Health Act 1983 [Crown Copyright 1983].

The Offences Against the Person Act 1861 [Crown Copyright 1861].

The Police and Criminal Evidence Act 1984 (Crown Copyright 1984].

The Protection from Harassment Act 1997 (Crown Copyright 1997].

The Sexual Offences Act 1956 [Crown Copyright 1956].

Draft Legislation

The Draft Children (Contact) and Adoption Bill [Crown Copyright 2005].

Case Law

Re H (A Minor) (Shared Residence) [1994] 1 FLR 717.

D v D (Shared Residence Order) (Court of Appeal; Dame Elizabeth Butler-Sloss (P) and Hale LJ; 20 November 2000) [2001] FIR 295.

A Father and A Mother v Their Two Children (B and C) (2004) EWHC 142 (FAM).

(Gillick v West Norfolk and Wisbech AHA [1986] AC 112 at 113).
Re L & Others (Court of Appeal; Dame Elizabeth Butler-Sloss; June 2000).

Statistics

Judicial Statistics Annual Report 2005 – revised version published 14 August 2006 [Crown Copyright 2006].

Judicial Statistics Annual Report 2004 [Crown Copyright 2004].

Judicial Statistics Annual Report 2003 [Crown Copyright 2003].

Judicial Statistics Annual Report 2002 [Crown Copyright 2002].

Home Office Publications

The Framework for the Assessment of Children in Need and their Families

[Crown Copyright 2000].

Working Together to Safeguard Children 2006. [Crown Copyright].

CAFCASS Service Principles and Standards March 2003. [Crown Copyright].

Department for Education and Skills

The National Standards for Under Eights' Day Care and Child Minding – Child Minding [Crown Copyright 2003].

The National Standards for Under Eights' Day Care and Child Minding - Full Day Care [Crown Copyright 2003].

National Standards for Under Eights' Day Care and Child Minding - Out of School Care [Crown Copyright 2003].

National Standards for Under Eights' Day Care and Child Minding – Creches [Crown Copyright 2003].

The National Standards for Under Eights' Day Care and Child Minding – Sessional Care [Crown Copyright 2003].

Other

The Victoria Climbié Inquiry. Report of an Inquiry by Lord Laming [Crown Copyright 2003].

Government Response to the Constitutional Affairs Select Committee Report: Family Justice: the operation of the family courts [Crown Copyright 2005].

USEFUL CONTACTS

British Association for Counselling and Psychotherapy. You can find a local therapist on their website: www.bacp.co.uk.

BPD Central. An excellent resource for partners of people with borderline personality disorder, and they have an email support group called Welcome to Oz. Website: www.bpdcentral.com.

British Psychological Society. You can find a specialist psychologist on their website. Their address is: St Andrews House, 48 Princess Road East, Leicester, LE1 7DR. Telephone: 0116 254 9568. Fax: 0116 247 0787. Website: www.bps.org.uk. Email address: enquiry@bps.org.uk.

CAFCASS. The Children and Family Court Advisory and Support Service. Website: www.CAFCASS.gov/uk.

ChildLine is the free helpline service for children and young people in the UK. Helpline: 0800 1111. Website: www.childline.org.uk.

Children's Legal Centre. The Centre operates the Child Law Advice Line. Website: www.childrenslegalcentre.com. Helpline: 0845 120 2948.

Department for Constitutional Affairs, Child Abduction Unit. This department deals with children taken to countries that have signed the 1980 Hague Convention on the Civil Aspects of International Child Abduction. Their address is: 81 Chancery Lane, London, WC2A 1DD.

Department for Education. Address enquiries to: The Family Division, DfES, Caxton House, Tothill St, London SW1H 9NA. Telephone: 0207 2731386.

Disability Rights Commission is an independent body established in April 2000 by Act of Parliament to stop discrimination and promote equality of opportunity for disabled people. Their website is www.drc.gov.uk. Helpline: 08457 622 633. Textphone: 08457 622 644. Their address is: DRC Helpline, FREEPOST MID02164, Stratford upon Avon, CV37 9BR.

Domestic Violence Helpline providing access to 24-hour emergency refuge accommodation as well as an information service, including safety planning and translation facilities to thousands of women who suffer at the hands of an abusive partner. Telephone: 0808 2000 247.

Families Need Fathers. Provides information and support to parents, including unmarried parents, of either sex. FNF is chiefly concerned with the problems of maintaining a child's relationship with both parents during and after family breakdown. Helpline: 08707 607496. Website: www.fnf. org.uk.

Family Mediation Helpline. Telephone: 0845 6026627. Website: www. familymediationhelpline.co.uk.

Family Rights Group. An independent charity providing help and advice to people whose children are involved with Social Services. Their address is: The Print House, 18 Ashwin Street, London E8 3DL. Helpline: 0800 731 1696. Website: www.frg.org.uk.

Foreign and Commonwealth Office. Their address is: King Charles Street, London, SW1A 2AH.

Her Majesty's Court Service. Website: www.hmCourts-service.gov.uk. Information Commissioner - England. The Information Commissioner can be contacted when you don't receive information that you're entitled to under Section 7 of the Data Protection Act. Website: www.ico.gov.uk. In England, write to: The Information Commissioner's Office, Wycliffe House, Water Lane, Wilmslow, Cheshire, SK9 5AF. Helpline: 01625 545 745. Fax: 01625 524 510. Email: mail@ico.gsi.gov.uk.

Information Commissioner – Wales. Wales has its own Information Commissioner. Write to: Information Commissioner's Office – Wales, 2 Alexandra Gate, Ffordd Pengam, Cardiff, CF24 2SA. Telephone: 02920 894 929. Fax: 02920 894 930.

Law Society of England and Wales. You can find a solicitor specialising in family mediation by contacting the Law Society, via their website (where you can search by geographic location) at: www.lawsociety.org.uk. Telephone: 0870 606 6575 (find a solicitor telephone service).

Legal Services Commission. The body responsible for administering legal aid. Their website includes an eligibility calculator under the Community Legal Services banner. Website www.legalservices.gov.uk.

Local Government Ombudsman. If you have a complaint about Social Services, the Ombudsman can act if Social Services have failed to investigate your complaint, or you disagree with their decision. Website: www.lgo.org.uk.

MALE Domestic Violence Helpline. Providing support and advice for male victims of domestic violence. Helpline: 0845 064 6800

Member of Parliament. A useful website which helps identify your Member of Parliament, and gives you contact details. Website: www. upmystreet.com.

Mental Health Trusts. A website listing all Mental Health Trusts. Website: www.nhs.uk/England/AuthoritiesTrusts/MentalHealth/list.aspx

MIND. Mind is the leading mental health charity in England and Wales, providing advice and information. Infoline: 0845 766 0163. Website: www. mind.org.uk.

National Association of Child Contact Centres is a national charity that supports over 325 Child Contact Centres throughout the British Isles (excluding Scotland). Their address is: Minerva House, Spaniel Row, Nottingham NG1 6EP. Telephone: 0845 4500 280. Fax: 0845 4500 420. Website: www.naccc.org.uk.

National Education Law Advice Line. Providing telephone advice about matters relating to children and education. Telephone: 0845 345 4345. Email: nel@essex.ac.uk.

NSPCC. (National Society for the Prevention of Cruelty to Children). Helpline: 0808 800 5000. Website: www.nspcc.org.uk.

Ofsted Early Years. Handle problems with playgroups and nurseries and non-adherence to the National Standards. Address complaints to: Ofsted, The CIE Team, 3rd Floor, Royal Exchange Buildings, St Ann's Square, Manchester, M2 7LA. Telephone: 0845 601 4772

Parentline Plus. Helpline: 0808 800 2222. Text Phone: 0800 783 6783. Webpage: www.parentlineplus.org.uk includes an email help service.

Passport Office can be contacted for advice about the prevention of passports being issued to children. Their address is: United Kingdom Passport Service, Caveats Section, Globe House, 89 Ecclestone Square, London, SWIV 1PN. Website: www.passport.gov.uk.

Primary Care Trusts. A useful website to locate your local Primary Care Trust to assist you in locating your child's General Practitioner. Website: www.nhs.uk/England/AuthoritiesTrusts/Pct/Default.aspx

The Principal Registry of the Family Division. The organisation responsible for registering parental responsibility. Their address: First Avenue House, 42-49 High Holborn, London WC1V 6NP.

The Private Family Law Team, Looked After Children Division, Department for Education and Skills. This department publishes the leaflet DfEE 0092/2000 'Schools, "Parents" and "Parental Responsibility"' providing guidance to Head Teachers of all schools in relation to their duty to include parents in their children's schooling. Their address is: Caxton House, Tothill Street, London SW1H 9NA.

Relate is the UK's largest provider of relationship counselling services. Website: www.relate.org.uk. To find a local counsellor call: 0845 456 1310. You can also arrange telephone counselling and advice by email from their website. There is a charge for this service which is detailed on their website.

Resolution first for family law. An association representing 5,000 solicitors who follow a code of practice aimed at constructive, non-confrontational dispute resolution. Website: www.sfla.org.uk.

Respect runs a telephone service providing information and advice for perpetrators of domestic violence, practitioners, partners and others who would like information. Telephone: 0845 122 8609.

Reunite is a UK charity recommended by the Foreign Office to help parents whose children have been abducted and taken abroad. Their address: P O Box 7124, Leicester, LE1 7XX. Website: www.reunite.org

Samaritans. Helpline: 08457 90 90 90. You can send texts to: 07725 90 90 90. You can also write, addressing letters to: Chris, P O Box 9090, Stirling, FK8 2SA. Send emails to: jo@samaritans.org. Website: www.samaritans.org.uk.

Saneline offers crisis and emotional support to people suffering from mental illness, and to their families, and can signpost you to local support resources. Helpline: 0845 767 8000. Website: www.sane.org.uk.

Tricho-Tech Limited. A forensic drug testing laboratory. Their address is: No.1 Pentwyn Business Centre, Cardiff, CF23 7HB. Telephone: 029 2054 0542. Fax: 029 2073 5036. Email address: info@tricho-tech.co.uk. Website: www.tricho-tech.co.uk.

UK College of Family Mediators. The UK College of Family Mediators sets standards for family mediation and maintains a register of family mediator members who meet these standards. Website www.ukcfm.co.uk. Their address is: Alexander House, Telephone Avenue, Bristol, BS1 4BS. Telephone: 0117 904 7223. Fax: 0117 904 3331.

Women's Aid Federation of England, P O Box 391, Bristol, BS99 7WS. Helpline: 0808 2000 247. Website: www.womensaid.org.uk. They also have an advice line for men who are victims of domestic violence. Helpline: 0845 064 8000.

END NOTES

[1]   *Part I, Section 1(1) of the Children Act 1989* states that "When a court determines any question with respect to (a) the upbringing of a child; or (b) the administration of a child's property or the application of any income arising from it, the child's welfare shall be the court's paramount consideration" (Crown Copyright 1989).

[2]   *The Judicial Statistics Annual Report 2004 Table 5.3 p.69*. This report records 137,954 Court Orders (including Parental Responsibility Orders) having been considered in private family law cases in 2003/4. *The Judicial Statistics Annual Report 2005 Table 5.3 p.67* records 117,071 Court Orders having been considered in 2004/5.

[3]   Legal Services Commission leaflet "*A Practical Guide to Community Legal Service Funding*" which can be found on their website.

[4]   *Section 3.13* of the Government guidelines '*the Framework for the Assessment of Children in Need and their Families*' (FACNF) sets out the right to see Social Services welfare reports on your children. These rights are also upheld in the *Data Protection Act 1998*. Social Services may only consider withholding information where disclosure of information would prejudice the prevention or detection of crime - *FACNF Appendix E Section 10*.

[5]   *The Children Act 1989 Section 9(7)*.

[6]   Private applications to the Court and the types of Court Order which can be made within Family Law are set out under *Section 8 of the Children Act 1989* and are known as *Section 8 Orders*.

[7]   *The Family Proceedings Rules 1991 Section 4.17* states that parties to legal proceedings are entitled to see a copy of statements, documented evidence and expert reports which will be presented to the Court.

[8]   *The Children Act 1989 Section 11*.

[9]   Section 15 of the Government Response to the Constitutional

Affairs Select Committee Report: Family Justice: the operation of the family courts [March 2005] stated that "The Government has long recognised that delay in reaching a resolution can have the effect of benefiting the resident parent and thus weaken the position of the non-resident parent." (Crown Copyright 2005).

10 *The Family Proceedings Courts (Miscellaneous Amendments) Rules 2005* and the *Family Proceedings (Amendment No 4) Rules 2005* are the two principle pieces of legislation that set out with whom you are allowed to discuss details of your Court case and the text of Court Orders.

11 *The Children Act 1989 Section 97* prevents anyone from publishing or causing to be published any material which may cause a child to be identified as being involved, or having been involved in Family Law proceedings in the Magistrate's Court. This includes restrictions to other forms of media other than print, including radio and television.

12 *The Children Act 1989 Section 1(3).*

13 *Section 8(1) of the Children Act 1989* which provides a simple description of each type of Section 8 order.

14 *The Children Act 1989 Section 10(4).*

15 Statistics show that less than 1% of applications for Contact Orders were refused by Courts between 2002 and 2005. (Source: *Judicial Statistics Annual Reports for 2002, 2003, 2004* and *2005*).

16 *The Children Act 1989 Section 13(1).*

17 *The Children Act 1989 Section 10(5).*

18 *The Children Act 1989 Section 10(10).*

19 *The Children Act 1989 Section 10(9).*

20 *The Children Act 1989 Section 10(8).*

21 *The Children Act 1989 Section 11(5).*

22 *The Children Act 1989 Section 13.*

23 *The Children Act 1989 Section 13(2).*

24   *The Children Act 1989 Guidance and Regulations, Volume 1, Court Orders (in paragraph 2.2(8), page 10)* published by the Stationery Office in 1991.

25   *H (A Minor) (Shared Residence) [1994] 1 FLR 717.*

26   *D v D (Shared Residence Order) (Court of Appeal; Dame Elizabeth Butler-Sloss (P) and Hale LJ; 20 November 2000) [2001] FIR 295.*

27   *A Father and A Mother v Their Two Children (B and C) (2004) EWHC 142 (FAM).*

28   *The Children Act 1989 Section 45(1).*

29   *The Children Act 1989 Section 45(5).*

30   *The Children Act 1989 Section 44(4)(a)* and *Section (44)(4)(b)(i).*

31   *The Children Act 1989 Section 44(4)(c).*

32   *The Children Act 1989 Section 44(6)* and *44(8).*

33   *The Family Law Act 1996 Schedule 6 Section 2(a)* including the revision to The Children Act 1989 including *Sections 44(a)(1), 44(a)(2), 44(a)(3) and 44(a)(5).*

34   *The Children Act 1989 Section 44(1).*

35   *The Children Act 1989 Section 44(4)(b)(ii).*

36   *The Children Act 1989 Section 45(8), Section 45(9),* and *Section 45(11).*

37   *The Children Act 1989 Section 47(1).*

38   *The Emergency Protection Order (Transfer of Responsibilities) Regulations 1991 Section 2.*

39   *The Emergency Protection Order (Transfer of Responsibilities) Regulations 1991 Section 3.*

40   *The Emergency Protection Order (Transfer of Responsibilities) Regulations 1991 Section 5.*

41   *The Children Act 1989 Section 50(1).*

42   *The Children Act 1989 Section 50(4)(a).*

43   *The Children Act 1989 Section 50(3).*

44   *The Children Act 1989 Section 50(9)* and *Section 50(10).*

45   *The Children Act 1989 Section 9(5)(a).*

46   *The Children Act 1989 Section 16(1)(b).*

47   *The Children Act 1989 Section 16(7).*

48   *The Children Act 1989 Section 16(2).*

49   *The Children Act 1989 Section 16(3).*

50   *The Children Act 1989 Section 16(5).*

51   *The Children Act 1989 Section 16(6).*

52   *The Family Law Act 1986 Section 34.*

53   *The Children Act 1989 Section 14(2).*

54   In the case *Churchard v Churchard [1984] FLR 635* – Lord Justice Ormrod stated that in cases involving breaches of orders relating to access, committal to prison was ultimately futile and shouldn't be used.

55   *The Draft Children (Contact) and Adoption Bill.*

56   *The Children Act 1989 Section 3(1).*

57   *The Children Act 1989 Section 3(4)(a).*

58   *The Children Act 1989 Section 2(7).*

59   *The Children Act 1989 Section 2 and Section 4.*

60   *The Adoption and Children Act 2002 Section 111.*

61   *The Judicial Statistics Annual Report 2004 Table 5.3 p.69. The Judicial Statistics Annual Report 2005 Table 5.3 p.67.*

62   *The Access to Health Records Act 1990 Section 3(1)(c).*

63   *The Access to Health Records Act 1990 Section 2(1).*

64   *The Access to Health Records Act 1990 Section 4(2).*

65   *The Access to Health Records Act 1990 Section 5(1)(a)(i).*

66   *The Access to Health Records Act 1990 Section 5(1)(a)(ii).*

67   In the case *Gillick v West Norfolk and Wisbech AHA [1986] AC*

112 at 113 [1985].

[68] *The Education Act 1996 Section 576.*

[69] *Schools, "Parents" and "Parental Responsibility' "* reference DfEE 0092/2000 [published by the Department for Education and Skills June 2000].

[70] *The National Standards for Under Eights' Day Care and Child Minding – Child Minding - Out of School Care. The National Standards for Under Eights' Day Care and Child Minding – Creches. The National Standards for Under Eights' Day Care and Child Minding – Sessional Care.* There is a statutory duty on Day Care and Child Minding providers to meet these standards under *The Day Care and Child Minding (National Standards) (England) Regulations 2003 Section 4(2)(b).*

[71] *The National Standards for Day Care Standard 12* [published by Ofsted 2001].

[72] *The Education (Pupil Information) (England) Regulations 2005 and The Education (Pupil Information) (Wales) Regulations 2004* entitle you to a copy of your children's educational record.

[73] *The Human Rights Act 1998 Article 9.*

[74] *The Children Act 1989 Section 13(1)(a).*

[75] *The Children Act 2004 Section 58.*

[76] *The Children Act 1989 Section 13(1) Section 13(1)(b)* and *Section 13(2).*

[77] *The Data Protection Act 1998 Section 7.*

[78] *The Children Act 1989 Section 7(1)(b)(i).*

[79] *The Children Act 1989 Section 7.*

[80] *The Children Act 1989 Section 7(5).*

[81] *The Children Act 1989 Section 47(1)(a)(i).*

[82] *The Framework for the Assessment of Children in Need and their Families* [published by the Department of Health April 2000].

83   *Service Principles and Standards* [published by the Children and Family Court Advisory and Support Service March 2003].

84   *The Family Proceedings Rules 1991 Section 4.13(2).*

85   *The Family Proceedings Rules 1991 Section 4.13(1).*

86   *The Criminal Justice and Court Service Act 2000 Section 16(1).*

87   CAFCASS Leaflet *'The Children and Family Report'* [CAFCASS V3-05 Leaflet]

88   *The Children Act 1989 Section 47(1)(b).*

89   *The Children Act 1989 Section 46.*

90   *The Children Act 1989 Section 46(6).*

91   *The Children Act 1989 Section 33(1).*

92   *The Children Act 1989 Section 35(1).*

93   *The Victoria Climbié Inquiry. Report of an Inquiry by Lord Laming,* Presented to Parliament by the Secretary of State for the Home Department by Command of Her Majesty January 2003.

94   *The Victoria Climbié Inquiry. Report of an Inquiry by Lord Laming, Recommendation 91.*

95   *The Children Act 1989 Section 31(9) as amended by Section 120 of The Adoption and Children Act 2002.*

96   *The Police and Criminal Evidence Act 1984 Section 17.*

97   *The Criminal Justice Act 1998 Section 39.*

98   *The Offences Against the Person Act 1861 Section 47.*

99   *The Criminal Damage Act 1971 Section 1(1).*

100   *The Protection from Harassment Act 1997 Section 2.*

101   *Sexual Offences Act 1956 Section 1(1), Section 14 and Section 15.*

102   *Metropolitan Police website: www.met.police.uk/dv/.*

103   *The Family Law Act 1996 Section 42(1).*

104   *The Family Law Act 1996 Section 33(3).*

105   In the case *Re M (Intractable Contact Dispute: Interim Care*

Order) (2003) 2 FLR 636.

[106] *The Mental Health Act 1983 Section 1(2).*

[107] *The Mental Health Act 1983 Section 2.*

[108] *The Mental Health Act 1983 Section 114.*

[109] *The Mental Health Act 1983 Section 3.*

[110] *The Mental Health Act Section 23.*

[111] In the case *Re M (Intractable Contact Dispute: Interim Care Order) (2003) 2 FLR 636.*

INDEX